D0061619

# Conducting Support Groups for Students Affected by Chemical Dependence

## A Guide for Educators and Other Professionals

**by Martin Fleming**
Edited by Cyril A. Reilly

JOHNSON INSTITUTE

Minneapolis 1990

Published by Johnson Institute Books
7151 Metro Blvd., Suite 250
Minneapolis, Minnesota 55435

**Library of Congress Cataloging-in-Publication Data**

Fleming, Martin
     Conducting support groups for students affected by chemical dependence.

     1. High school students—United States—Drug use. 2. Narcotic addicts—Counseling of—United States. 3. High School Students—Counseling of—United States. 4. Self-help groups—United States. I Title.
HV5824.Y68F59  1990          373.17'84          89-26718
ISBN 0-935908-51-X

To all young people struggling with the effects of chemical dependence who haven't yet found their way.

## Acknowledgments

I would like to thank Carole Remboldt of the Johnson Institute for her helpful direction and advice, Cyril A. Reilly for his fine editing, and Dick Schaefer for being there from the beginning. And to all the students and caregivers whom I have had the privilege of working with, a heartfelt thanks. Our experiences together are the foundation of this book.

# Contents

Introduction .................................................................................. 1

**1. How Chemical Dependence
Affects Three Kinds of Students** ........................................ 9
The Student with a Chemically Dependent Parent ............... 11
The Student Who Is Abusing Chemicals ................................ 12
The Recovering Chemically Dependent Student................... 13

**2. Functions and Design of a Support Group:
An Overview** ......................................................................... 15
Function 1: Fostering Insight .............................................. 16
Function 2: Providing Support ........................................... 16
Design ..................................................................................... 17

**3. Issues Central to Each Kind of Support Group** ............... 23
Concerned Persons Group .................................................... 24
Drug Information Group ....................................................... 25
Recovery Group ..................................................................... 27

**4. Starting an Initial Support Group** ................................... 31
The Ideal Number of Students ............................................ 32
Scheduling .............................................................................. 32
Parental Consent ................................................................... 33
Confidentiality ...................................................................... 34
Policies on Physical and Sexual Abuse .............................. 35
Closed Group vs. Open Group ............................................ 36
The Group Room ................................................................... 37
Basic Rules for the Group ................................................... 38

Addendum 4.1: Group Schedule ......................................... 41
Addendum 4.2a: Rules for a Concerned Persons Group........ 42
Addendum 4.2b: Rules for a Drug Information Group .......... 43
Addendum 4.2c: Rules for a Recovery Group ...................... 44
Addendum 4.3: Letter to Parents ......................................... 45

**5. Building a Support-Group Program** ........................................... 47
Evolution of a Typical Support-Group Program ...................... 48
Obtaining Administration Approval ........................................ 49
Appointing a Support-Group Coordinator ............................. 52
Involving Other Educators ....................................................... 52
Involving the Community ......................................................... 53
Choosing Group Leaders .......................................................... 54
Training Group Leaders ............................................................ 59
Providing Support for Group Leaders .................................... 61
Deciding on the Number of Leaders in a Group ..................... 62
Finding Time to Lead Support Groups .................................... 63

Addendum 5: Survey of Chemical Use .................................... 64

**6. Strengths Needed in a Group Leader** ....................................... 67
Knowing Your Community Resources ..................................... 67
Improving Your Group Skills and
    Knowledge of Chemical Dependence ................................. 68
Resolving Behavior Problems in a Group ............................... 69
Being Compassionate ................................................................ 71
Clearing Up Your Personal Problems ...................................... 71
Establishing and Maintaining
    Leader/Student Boundaries ................................................ 72
Having a Personal Support System .......................................... 73

**7. Finding Students for a Support Group** ................................... 75
Publicity ..................................................................................... 76
Building a Referral Network ..................................................... 76
Membership Criteria ................................................................. 79

Addendum 7: Confidential Questionnaire ............................. 82

**8. Format for Each Kind of Support Group** ............................85
  Activities Common to All Three Groups ......................87
  Format for a Concerned Persons Group ......................88
  Format for a Drug Information Group ......................104
  Format for a Recovery Group ................................111

  Addendum 8.1: Session Outline ..............................114
  Addendum 8.2: Warm-ups ....................................115
  Addendum 8.3: Interview Activity ..........................117
  Addendum 8.4: My Own Feelings .............................119
  Addendum 8.5: Ten Feelings ................................120
  Addendum 8.6: My Own Needs ................................121
  Addendum 8.7: From Now On ..................................122
  Addendum 8.8: History of My Chemical Use .................123
  Addendum 8.9: Chemicals and Feelings .....................125
  Addendum 8.10: Chemicals and Defenses ....................127
  Addendum 8.11: Survival Roles of Children from
    Families Affected by Chemical Dependence ...............131

**9. What Happens After the Group Disbands?** ...........................135
  Evaluating Individual Group Members .......................135
  Concerned Persons Group: Recommendations .................137
  Drug Information Group: Recommendations ..................138
  Recovery Group: Recommendations ..........................139
  Evaluating the Group .......................................139

  Addendum 9: Support-Group Feedback .......................141

**Afterword** ...............................................................143
**Resources** ..............................................................144
**Appendix: The Twelve Steps** .............................................152

# Introduction

Yesterday as I sat with a fifteen-year-old student, I watched tears trail down his cheeks as he attempted to hold back the feelings threatening to emerge after years of silence. Finally the words did come—words describing feelings of anger, fear, and love for a father with a drinking problem.

The next class period a different sort of student wandered into my office. She wore an army jacket with the sleeves cut out, she had drawn a large pot leaf on her notebook, and she looked tired and listless but at the same time defiant. Many of her teachers had approached me with concerns about her: Her grades had dropped dramatically, she was often absent, her circle of friends had a reputation for using drugs, and she often smelled of marijuana. I asked her about this, but she denied it all. "I don't care about school, I've been sick lately, and I've gotten high only once or twice in my whole life," she told me. So I asked her to explain how it was that she had been caught smoking pot during her lunch break. "That school rent-a-cop is always trying to bust me and my friends," she said, slumping down further in her chair. It was obvious to me that she wasn't willing to take an honest look at the damage her chemical abuse was causing her.

That afternoon I met with a student who had been back in school for only a few days since completing a treatment program for chemical dependence. He seemed scared and hesitant.

1

Wearing his recent sobriety like a stiff new suit, he told me that his old drug-using friends were already approaching him in the halls and that he didn't know how to respond. I wondered if he'd be among those who stay straight.

These three typify the three groups of students in our schools who need special help: students worn down by the damaging effects of a parent's drinking problem, students who are themselves abusing chemicals, and students in recovery, struggling not to use alcohol and other drugs anymore. These three groups exist in every school across the nation. It's obvious that they need help, but should schools be getting involved?

Of course they should. Schools already provide many kinds of help to correct problems that interfere with students' ability to learn: for instance, special education classes for the emotionally or behaviorally handicapped, remedial reading courses and other assistance for those who are visually or auditorially impaired. But chemical abuse or dependence also interferes with the learning process; students caught up in it generally experience lower grade-point averages, higher dropout rates, and impaired social functioning. So why shouldn't schools help? Without some sort of special help, these students become adults who give birth to the next generation of chemically dependent adolescents.

Schools alone can't solve the many complex problems associated with the disease of chemical dependence. But they can do a great deal. This book proposes just one kind of practical, effective way in which educators can tackle the problem: **Start support groups** for these three kinds of students struggling with chemical dependence. I suggest these support groups not as a complete program but as one component of a wide-ranging Student Assistance Program (SAP) that covers all aspects of the chemical-abuse problem: education/prevention, identification, early intervention, referral, counseling, support groups, and knowledgeable, active involvement of the administration, the entire school staff, students, parents, and the larger civic community. A fully functioning Student Assistance Program creates a schoolwide climate of chemical (alcohol/other drug) awareness, healthy attitudes, and acceptable norms for behavior. And it goes beyond problems with chemicals to help students who are experiencing other types of personal, family, or performance/behavior problems. (An excellent SAP Program manual is listed in Resources.)*

My own experience, as well as that of many colleagues, convinces me both that such support groups are desperately needed and that they can be successful. Here's why I make that double claim.

First, these three groups of students need accurate information and a forum where they can discuss their personal problems. Support groups provide that opportunity. Students affected by chemical dependence, whether their own or someone else's, need accurate, age-appropriate information about mind-altering chemicals and their effects, and they need opportunities to discuss and apply this information to their own lives. Schools are already in the business of providing information and opportunities for discussion. Certainly they can supply a safe, supportive environment outside the traditional classroom where support groups can meet. But students who are already affected need a teaching vehicle different from the traditional classroom. Working in a small group setting is the answer.

Groups provide the safety and confidentiality that students (or anyone for that matter) need in order to talk about personal problems they're experiencing. It's through these experiences that personal growth and healing take place. When students are preoccupied with last night's drunken fight between their parents, they now have the opportunity to share that with

---

* For more information, see *When Chemicals Come to School: The Student Assistance Program Manual* by Gary L. Anderson in Resources.

others and to receive helpful information about what they can do to take care of themselves. Students in trouble with their own chemical use can now be effectively confronted and given the opportunity to deal with their problem. And when students in recovery are struggling to stay straight but are feeling vulnerable to chemicals, they now have a place where they can reach out and get support from peers who have experienced similar difficulties.

Secondly, educators need support groups. So many students are affected by chemical dependence that the one or two counselors in a school can barely make a dent in the problem. But in a small group, a group leader can assist seven students in the same amount of time he or she would normally devote to one student. Support groups bring a manageable solution to the problem of overwhelming numbers. They also provide constructive peer pressure that's absent in individual counseling with adults, and they encourage students to learn from each other, a technique that has proven to be very effective.

Thirdly, support groups have been successful in schools because they're easily within the capabilities of concerned and experienced educators. While some additional training for leading groups is necessary, being a therapist or a counselor is definitely not necessary. Support groups don't involve therapy—they are **support** groups. Educators, administrators, community volunteers—many people from a variety of backgrounds can become excellent group leaders, given the right motivation and assistance.

Convinced by my own and others' experience that support groups are needed and can succeed in our schools, I wrote this book to show you how to start and then coordinate such groups. You'll find this book easy to understand and easy to use—a real how-to book. Here's a brief preview of what it does.

Chapter 1 clarifies the effects of chemical dependence. Chapter 2 discusses the major goals of a support group and briefly explains how a carefully designed format helps the group attain those goals. Chapter 3 describes the three basic types of student support groups: a Concerned Persons Group, for students affected by someone else's chemical dependence; a Drug Information Group, for students who are abusing chemicals; and a Recovery Group, for chemically dependent students who have quit on their own or who have been in treatment and are working on sobriety.

Chapter 4 provides the practical information you'll need to start a support group yourself; it offers solutions to such problems as scheduling, parental consent, and basic rules for a support group. When a single support group grows into several support groups, a managing structure becomes necessary. So Chapter 5 outlines a support-group program: It discusses how to get administrative approval, get a coordinator, involve other educators and the larger community, how to choose, train, and support the group leaders, and how to find time to lead groups.

Chapter 6 discusses the strengths a group leader needs.

Students affected by chemical dependence are often difficult to identify. Most students so affected won't advertise this fact, which makes it hard to find students appropriate for a support group. So Chapter 7 discusses several different strategies for finding these students.

The heart of the book is Chapter 8. Three separate formats, one for each type of support group, are outlined and then discussed at length—step-by-step, week-by-week. Beginning group leaders will be able to start a support group right away by following these formats. These formats are effective, practical instruments for providing the information and the opportunities for discussion and interaction that students need in order to learn about themselves and to recover from the effects of chemical dependence.

Chapter 9 discusses what to do when a support group is finished, including how to evaluate each group member and the support group as a whole.

The Addenda found at the end of many chapters will be of great practical help; they include questionnaires, activities, and much other useful material. (By the way, a reference such as Addendum 8.3 directs you to Chapter 8, Addendum 3; a reference such as Addendum 5 directs you to the one Addendum found at the end of Chapter 5.)

At the end of the book you'll find a quite extensive list of Resources: outstanding books, workbooks, booklets, films/videocassettes, and names and addresses of national organizations important in the field of chemical dependence. An Appendix reprints the famous Twelve Steps of Alcoholics Anonymous.

This book is designed to benefit young persons from grades seven through twelve. While there are differences in maturity and cognitive levels with this range of students, the activities and concepts are general enough so that you can easily make adjustments to meet your own students' needs.

If your school doesn't yet have a Student Assistance Program in place, you'll be happy to know that such system-wide programs do tend to be implemented as a result of the successful work that's done in even one support group. Any start is a good beginning. All it takes to get started is motivated and reasonably informed educators, school counselors, or other caregivers, such as yourself, who want to start a support group for students. First you can start a single group, then add a few more until some kind of coordinating effort is necessary; eventually, we hope, you'll arrive at a comprehensive SAP.

The ideas and group formats in this book can be implemented immediately. These are time-tested and field-tested techniques based on eight years' experience developing support-group programs similar to the one outlined in this book. Through leading countless support groups, I've learned a great deal from the students struggling to understand and recover from the effects of chemical dependence and have benefited personally from being able to be part of that process.

My own work with support groups in schools was born of an underlying belief that young people affected by chemical dependence need to talk about what they're feeling and be offered support so that they can make positive changes in their lives. It's a simple goal, and yet many students still don't have this opportunity.

I know that I certainly didn't. At one time I was a hurting, confused, chemically dependent adolescent. I ran away from home regularly, skipped school often, and smoked pot every day. I desperately needed someone to talk to. But with the exception of one teacher, no one ever offered any help. Ever. Even when I finally got some help, graduated from a chemical dependence treatment program, and returned to school, there still wasn't any kind of support group available. In those days few chemically dependent adolescents successfully made the transition to sobriety.

That was in the 1970s. The situation is finally changing. Schools are beginning to acknowledge the problem and are offering help to such students. My goal, my mission, has been to provide opportunities for such students to recover from the damaging effects of chemical dependence by providing support groups.

But I'm only one person working in a single school. Support groups are needed in every school. This book, combined with your own insights, will provide you with the necessary tools to establish support groups in your school, for your students. It's time to get started.

*Chapter 1*

# How Chemical Dependence Affects Three Kinds of Students

Since the beginning of recorded time adult humans have used various chemicals to alter their minds and feelings.* And throughout history a certain percentage of those people have become dependent on those mind-altering chemicals, with predictable results: personal heartache, wasted potential, broken relationships. What's relatively recent, however, is the use of mind-altering chemicals by adolescents. Even before young people in our society reach their teenage years, they're feeling social pressure that forces them to make choices about whether

---

* **Note:** I use the term "chemicals" throughout this book to refer to **all** mind-altering drugs, including alcohol. I also use the term "chemical dependence" because it covers addiction to all mind-altering drugs and because it's short and simple. I do want to emphasize that alcohol **is** a drug—just like cocaine, marijuana, uppers, downers, or any other mind-altering drug. Too often people talk about "alcohol or drugs" or "alcohol and drugs" as if alcohol were somehow different from drugs and in a category by itself. True, our culture, our government, even our laws, treat alcohol differently from the way they treat other drugs such as pot, crack, or smack. But the symptoms of addiction are essentially the same for all these mind-altering drugs, and the need to find ways to prevent or intervene with their use is just as urgent.

to use alcohol or other drugs. Chemical use, abuse, and dependence are now entrenched problems in the lives of school-age children, and the primary battleground where these problems manifest themselves is the school.

In a typical classroom, then, we'll find three kinds of students much affected by chemical dependence—the three kinds this book deals with. Some are preoccupied with thoughts of their parents or other family members who are chemically dependent (though for brevity's sake, from now on we'll simply refer to chemically dependent parents). Some are themselves abusing chemicals. And some are in recovery—chemically dependent students who have either quit on their own or who have been in a treatment program and are now struggling to stay straight.

These young people carry their problems with them wherever they go, of course. But this book concentrates on their school life, which is their present calling and where they're heavily influenced by their peers. At school, educators see firsthand the devastating effects of chemical dependence on students: behavior problems, lack of motivation, poor attendance, poor grades. Every day they witness the sad reality of wasted potential and the legacy of chemical dependence being passed from generation to generation.

These three kinds of students are very different from one another in the way they're affected by chemical dependence, so we'll discuss them one by one. This discussion will pave the way for presenting the three types of support groups we advocate in this book: the Concerned Persons Group, for those students affected by parental chemical dependence; the Drug Information Group, for those who are themselves abusing chemicals; and the Recovery Group.

## The Student With A Chemically Dependent Parent

Students with chemically dependent parents aren't usually identified as such by educators. They're the silent victims and are among the hidden costs of chemical dependence. Even when educators do notice the behavioral or emotional problems of such students, they often don't associate those problems with parental chemical dependence.

Yet an estimated 28 million Americans feel the effects of parental chemical dependence—and 12 to 15 million of these are students.* This means that one out of four students in a typical classroom has a chemically dependent parent or parents.

One of the more immediate effects of parental chemical dependence on students is preoccupation. A student might be labeled a "daydreamer" or told that he can't "stay on task." In reality, he's probably preoccupied with thoughts of his chemically dependent mother at home alone. He worries that she'll accidentally start the house on fire or neglect his baby sister. Another student plays over in her mind the fight at the dinner table the night before and wonders where the family will be moving now that Dad has lost yet another job because of his drinking.

A chemically dependent environment produces children who often have feelings of low self-worth, depression, poor communication skills, hostility, and various other problems with relationships. As students they'll sometimes have severe behavior problems and will be prone to anxiety, learning disabilities, or attention-deficit disorders. Others will be compulsive over-achievers who become frantic at the thought of a less-than-perfect test score. As a whole, however, students

---

*See the article "Innocent Bystanders at Risk: The Children of Alcoholics" by Claudia Black, in *Alcoholism*, Jan.-Feb. 1981, pp. 22-26.

with chemically dependent parents don't perform as well in school as their peers.

Most often there are no publicly demonstrated behavior problems. Affected students hide the family secrets quite well. But even when these students seem well adjusted, the negative effects I've mentioned (and others as well) can be subtle and deep-rooted.

These children are also at high risk for developing chemical dependence themselves. If they don't become chemically dependent, they'll often marry someone who is. In either case, a new generation of children who will be harmfully affected by a parent's chemical dependence is almost assured.

## The Student Who Is Abusing Chemicals

Students who are chemically dependent use their drug of choice repeatedly even though it causes problems for them. It's not that such students are unintelligent or don't see the problems; it's that these mind-altering chemicals temporarily satisfy some basic needs. The chemicals make them feel good, numb their emotional pain, fill empty time, and establish them in a drug-using peer group. But chemicals can also hurt their bodies, create an emotional hell, ensure much empty time, and alienate them from friends and family.

For chemically dependent students, drugs—not their families, friends, schoolwork, or career—become the main focus of their lives. The chemically dependent student's priority is mind-altering chemicals and all that goes with them: the peer group, the parties, the "us against them" mentality, the excitement. School isn't part of this picture. Homework assignments aren't completed, grades deteriorate, classes are skipped, and motivation fades away. Feeling the effects of these depressing consequences, the chemically dependent student turns to the chemicals even more frequently for relief. Eventually there may be fights, suspensions, dropping out of school, verbal battles with parents, encounters with the police, health problems, even suicide.

## The Recovering Chemically Dependent Student

Even when students in recovery have stopped using chemicals, they still have problems. While these students usually have the best of intentions and much new-found energy after completing a treatment program, developmentally they're still at the age at which they started using chemicals. This means they probably have retarded social skills, among other problems. Returning to school and facing the academic problems they had before treatment can be overwhelming. Moreover, they can't fall back on their familiar coping mechanism—getting high.

*Chapter 2*

# Functions and Design of a Support Group: An Overview

The overall goal of a school-based chemical dependence support group is to help students who are affected by the disease of chemical dependence. More specifically, the goals include the following: to reduce feelings of loneliness and isolation by providing a sense of community; to develop an understanding of chemical dependence as a disease; to identify self-defeating behaviors and attitudes; to learn how to identify and express feelings; to provide encouragement, support, and nurturing; to alleviate feelings of shame; and to increase self-awareness and self-esteem. These goals are achieved by focusing on two primary functions of a support group: providing opportunities for members to gain insight, and giving support. After discussing those two functions briefly, we'll discuss major features of the design for ensuring that a support group reaches its goals.

## Function 1: Fostering Insight

Students affected by chemical dependence usually understand little about its nature and effects, and often the information they do have is incorrect. They gain new insight by absorbing the information presented by the group leader and by observing and listening to other members of their group. For example, if the group leader shows a film that highlights various ways in which chemical dependence affects children, it can begin to dawn on group members that many of their feelings are reactions to their parents' chemical dependence. Or perhaps a student gains new insight by observing a defensive group member deny that she has any problems with her chemical use even though everyone else in the group knows that the reason she's flunking this semester is that she's out drinking beer with her friends instead of going to class.

## Function 2: Providing Support

But insight alone isn't enough. Many cigarette smokers are aware that smoking is ruining their health, and yet they continue smoking. The students need support: They need to be encouraged to turn insight into action by changing their thoughts, feelings, attitudes, and behaviors. When students who haven't made the jump from insight to action see their peers making these changes, and when the leader and other group members encourage them to join the group, they'll tend to join and follow suit.

For example, when students in a support group talk about how they've been affected by someone else's chemical dependence and tell what they're doing to change things for themselves, the group member who's afraid to talk about his feelings because it's uncomfortable and because others might laugh will join in. And the more he talks, the easier it gets because nobody does laugh and everyone encourages him and tells him they've felt that way too.

Or think of a group member in recovery who already knows she should be staying sober but is often tempted to start using chemicals again. Every week she can talk about how the past week went and can mention that even though it was tough, she stayed sober. The group congratulates her and tells her to hang in there. Without such support she might soon start to use again.


## Design

Insight and support don't just happen by accident. They're attained by using the well-designed format presented in this book. Following this format, group leaders present new topics, steer the discussion, and provide the rules and authority that support-group members can count on. This total book provides you with the various tools you'll need to reach your group goals; this section simply explains **the main outlines** of the design and how it works.

An effective working group needs a solid foundation that includes a regular meeting time and place in a private group room, a small number of group members (between five and eight is ideal), a set of ground rules that protect group members and set limits, and a leader to guide the group process. (Building this foundation is discussed more fully in Chapter 4.)

With this foundation, the group will begin to evolve. It usually will start out as a collection of nervous, quiet students— definitely not a working group yet. At first they'll sit back in their chairs and laugh and volunteer only surface information about themselves. Through the use of various activities, though, the group will start to relax and open up. As the sessions continue, students are encouraged to take the risk of sharing feelings they usually wouldn't share in school halls or perhaps even with close friends. As they do so, the group begins to achieve true intimacy. And this openness and intimacy in turn help them gain new insights into themselves and their problems with chemicals.

When a support group reaches this point, wonderful things begin to happen. Anyone who has been through a treatment program will attest that the single most important aspect of the program was "my group." The intimacy and the bonding that take place in a support group are what set this type of group apart from other collective experiences. Adolescents, like all of us, ache for intimacy—for a real, lasting connection with other human beings. Mind-altering chemicals provide a cheap, illusory substitute for this experience that, sad to say, many people don't seem to have access to.

Each group session contains more than just a discussion of a specific topic. Typically a session starts with an activity before the session's main topic is introduced. After the students have discussed how this topic applies to them, the session closes with another brief activity.

The opening activity can be a brief warm-up question such as "What are you feeling right now?" or "Which feeling is the most difficult for you to express to others?" Such an opening is a quick, simple way to release students from preoccupation with the hustle and bustle of their everyday lives; it helps them focus on the group process—not unlike the way a runner stretches before a run.

After the warm-up, the leader introduces the main topic—for instance, by giving a brief lecture on chemical dependence or on the importance of expressing feelings. Sometimes instead of giving a lecture the leader might take an altogether different approach by initiating an activity—for instance, having students draw on paper a time when their chemically dependent

18

parents embarrassed other family members at the dinner table, or what it felt like to sit in their bedrooms listening to their parents fight. After the lecture or other activity, members are asked to relate this new information to their own lives and to share this insight with the group. This is awareness and support in action—gaining personal insight through the new information presented, listening to other group members share, and taking the risk to share one's own thoughts and feelings.

If a group warm-up can be compared to the stretching before a runner's workout, the group's closing activity could be compared to a runner's warm-down. Many times in a group the activity or discussion topic evokes raw feelings. It's important to gradually bring about some closure to the session rather than abruptly ending it when the bell rings. To facilitate this, the group might hold hands in a circle, shut their eyes, and imagine the love from their friends and family as the warm sun shining down on them. If one member is having a difficult time—for example, when she remembers being told that she was stupid and that no one liked her—the rest of the group might take turns telling her something about her that they really like or admire.

A couple of reminders are in order here. First, support groups don't always give students the warm, nurturing experiences that students enjoy—nor were they meant to do so. Sometimes—especially in groups for those abusing chemicals—confrontation is deliberately initiated by the group leader or other students. After all, these groups are designed to make the members look at aspects of their lives that they'd rather leave alone. A student might be stubbornly clinging to the delusion that she doesn't have a problem with her chemical use—until the rest of the group points out to her the discrepancy between what she's saying and the specific problems her chemical use is causing her. The group might remind her that her parents have kicked her out of the house because she came home drunk one too many times and that now she's living at a friend's house.

It's important to note that confrontation doesn't mean angry accusation, judgment, or negative criticism. In a support group it means pointing out the discrepancy between a person's words and actions—actions including body language. For example, a student might say, "I don't want to use," but keeps right on going to parties where everyone is using. Or students might respond that they aren't angry when, in fact, they have their arms folded tightly across their chests or are scowling. Confrontation isn't accusation; it means pointing out the facts.

As in any intimate gathering of people, there can be conflict. One student might accuse another of always monopolizing the discussion; another might complain that some people in the group aren't being honest. This is to be expected. Conflict is a stage of group development and is an indication of growing group intimacy.*

Some issues aren't appropriate for a support group. If a student reveals that she has been physically or sexually abused, for example, a support group wouldn't be the place to work on this issue; the student should be referred to a therapist. Likewise, there will be occasions when students are experiencing such extreme difficulty in their personal lives that a support group simply won't be enough. They need the professional assistance that only individual counseling can offer.

Regardless of whether the mood in the group is nurturing, playful, or tense, support groups provide the setting for students to gain insight and support: what they're feeling, why they do the things they do, and how they can change. The leader

---

* For more information about an excellent discussion of the stages of group development, see pages 133-139 of *From Peer Pressure to Peer Support* by Shelley MacKay Freeman in Resources.

can guide the process and introduce new information, but the interactions of the members—peer modeling, friendships, disclosing, nurturing—are the experiences that set support groups apart from other types of educational experiences.

*Chapter 3*

# Issues Central to Each Kind of Support Group

It would be naive to think that all one needs to do is gather a number of students affected by chemical dependence and say, "Okay, let's form a group." Many potential group members function in separate social circles and therefore don't work well together. Frequently, students with chemically dependent parents are over-achievers; consequently they don't mix well with the "druggie" crowd, who usually do poorly in school. Moreover, chemically dependent students who are in recovery are often reluctant to talk openly about their problems in the presence of students who can't wait until three o'clock to get drunk or stoned. For these and other reasons, it's best to have separate groups that focus on the specific issues characteristic of each of the three kinds of students. The divisions are straight-forward and logical: students affected by a family member's chemical dependence, students who are currently abusing chemicals, and students recovering from chemical dependence.

Discussion of these three types of support groups forms the backbone of this chapter and this book.

## Concerned Persons Group

Recognizing that a large number of students are harmfully affected by parental chemical dependence, many schools are beginning to provide support groups specifically targeted for these students. The problems that students bring to a Concerned Persons Group are more complex than those of the other groups. While the other two groups focus specifically on stopping the use of mind-altering chemicals, the Concerned Persons Group must address a wide variety of problems including low self-esteem, coping skills, physical or sexual abuse, and recognizing and sharing feelings. Hence this group usually requires at least twelve sessions.

On the surface, many students in such a group may seem to have little in common. Some will be among the school's best students, others among the worst. Some will be popular and have many friends, and some are social outcasts. But as you get to know these students you'll discover that they share similar basic circumstances: Their lives have been harmfully affected by someone else's chemical dependence.

Although the typical student will be one whose father or mother is chemically dependent, some will participate in a group because of a sibling's, grandparent's, or other relative's chemical dependence. Most of these students have rarely discussed this issue with others (some have never mentioned it to anyone), so this group takes a while to warm up. Once the students feel safe and have been encouraged to talk about their "family secrets," however, the group begins to open up.

The initial phase of this group builds trust and explores common problems the members are experiencing. The leader might ask the members to draw pictures of their lives, including the effects the chemically dependent parent has had on the family and the struggles they've experienced. For example, asking them to draw their families can identify how students place themselves in relation to other family members—whether close or distant. These relationships can then be explored to identify the students' feelings.

In later sessions, the leader provides information about chemical dependence so that members can try to understand their parents' drinking or other drug-using behavior. Since most students live with the chemically dependent person, group members are encouraged to devise personal coping strategies. Such strategies range from asking friends to lend a supportive ear, to identifying a relative's house where the student could stay when things get particularily abusive at home.

Leading a Concerned Persons Group is personally rewarding. In these groups you'll see students who have felt helpless and ashamed begin to learn about their feelings and how to take care of themselves. And these students will amaze you as they put into practice what they've learned.


## Drug Information Group

Students who are abusing chemicals should join a Drug Information Group. The hope is that they'll either quit using chemicals or, if need be, move into an intensive and structured program that will bring about the needed changes. A Drug Information Group is structured to teach the students about chemical abuse and dependence, encourage them to make a self-assessment, and help them make positive changes based on what they've learned about themselves and about chemical dependence.

A typical Drug Information Group lasts from six to eight sessions, each session presenting a different aspect of chemical use and dependence. Since most students deny they have a problem, reality is presented to them through discussions, worksheets, activities, and films. Awareness of the true extent of their chemical use gradually evolves. They're motivated to make healthy changes through positive peer pressure, presentation of constructive alternatives to continued abuse, and abstinence contracts with parents and the school.

At first glance, the students in a Drug Information Group might seem to be a bizarre assortment of misfits and rebels. Students in this group will have widely differing histories of chemical use. Some will have had little previous experience; they just happened to get caught (although this is what most of them say). Others, whose lives are now falling apart, will probably have a history of chemical abuse that stretches back to grade school. The group will also involve students from diverse socioeconomic backgrounds who have different attitudes, interests, dress styles, and drugs of choice.

Regardless of those differences, all members of the group share at least three things: They abuse chemicals, somebody found out, and people are concerned about them.

Although an occasional student might join a Drug Information Group voluntarily because his or her life is just plain miserable, usually there's some external pressure. Most often the student was caught in possession of or under the influence of mind-altering chemicals, or there was a referral from parents, school, or community agency. This pressure is important because it helps ensure regular attendance.

Two predominant behaviors characterize the members of a Drug Information Group: denial and resistance. Asking students why they're in a group usually evokes answers like "I don't have a problem with chemicals. My parents, the school, and the cops—they're my problem!" They often view the support group, and the teachers or other adults leading it, as threatening the one thing that works for them—getting high. Many group members will be angry that they have to participate, and they tend to project those angry feelings onto the group leader. The leader is seen as the bad guy, the one who's going to try to get them to quit using chemicals. While some of these groups will be enjoyable, others will be quite trying and exhausting for group leaders.

Even so, these groups are important and effective: important, because students abusing chemicals need to be confronted before they'll change; and effective, because the changes **do** happen. Whether these students stop abusing mind-altering chemicals on their own or enter a more structured environment that will bring that about, a Drug Information Group will have a positive effect on their lives.


## Recovery Group

Most schools have at least a small number of students who have been in a chemical dependence treatment program and are struggling to meet the demands of a recovery program. Nearly all of these students will be chemically free during and immediately after their treatment program. Unfortunately, some won't remain abstinent. They come back to school still wearing the label of "druggie," and the school doesn't expect to see a different profile. On their first day back, old friends may ask them to go to a party that night, and they have to face the fact that nothing around them has changed. Providing a support group specifically for these students is crucial; it can mean the difference between a student's maintaining abstinence and starting to use chemicals again.

Although students have a variety of personal reasons for being in this group, their main goal is to stay sober. Most professionals believe that chemically dependent students need to maintain **total abstinence** from mind-altering chemicals in order to get their lives back on track. Usually, if they start to drink or get high again, their lives fall apart quickly.

Issues other than sobriety are discussed in a Recovery Group, however. These include lack of parental trust, the inability to say no to peers, sexuality issues, and parental chemical dependence. Applying new living skills acquired while in treatment can be both exciting and overwhelming for these students, so most of them will need support and feedback as they begin this process.

Perhaps the greatest stumbling block for these students is peer pressure. Students returning from an inpatient treatment program are concerned about what their friends are going to say. They want to know how they should respond when asked questions such as "Where have you been this past month?" or "So you're going to be a good little boy from now on?" Because students in recovery have broken away from their former drug-using friends and because their reputation excludes them from other peer groups, they'll usually be confronted with two unpleasant choices: either being abstinent and alone, or using chemicals and once again being accepted by their old friends. But getting them into a Recovery Group that meets each week throughout the school year provides a third choice that will keep many group members from falling back into familiar destructive patterns.

The atmosphere in a Recovery Group is different from that in other kinds of groups. Since most of these students have completed an intensive chemical dependence treatment program where they developed sophisticated communication skills, these groups move to an advanced level more quickly than other groups do.

In a healthy Recovery Group the students are comfortable talking about the personal details of their lives and helping other members who might not be doing so well. Usually many members of this group are also involved in ongoing therapy groups such as those in a mental health center or in a treatment center's aftercare program. They're usually attending Alcoholics Anonymous or Narcotics Anonymous as well. All in all, most members of a well-run Recovery Group are making positive and courageous changes in their lives, and being a part of this group can be exciting and personally rewarding for everyone involved.

*Chapter 4*

# Starting an Initial Support Group

Before you can start a support group you must address certain issues such as the number of students in your group, scheduling decisions, and confidentiality rules. This chapter will point out these problems and provide practical solutions.

After you've done most of the support-group planning but before you actually start the group, you should obtain at least informal approval from the administration to begin. By then you'll know enough about support groups to be able to explain to the administration what such groups are all about. (Chapter 5 discusses more fully how to prepare to meet with the administration to get formal approval to start a support-group **program**. That meeting will come when several groups have been working successfully and now need to be coordinated and given that formal approval. I repeat here that the support-group program should in turn be part of a much wider-ranging Student Assistance Program.)

## The Ideal Number of Students

Large support groups tend to be cognitive and discussion-oriented; small support groups encourage honest sharing of feelings. Five to eight students make an ideal-sized support group. Fewer than four don't create the kind of dynamic interaction that a somewhat larger support group does, and more than eight make it difficult for each student to share frequently. When you have many students wanting to join a support group, either start enough groups so that there's a manageable number in each, or decide to work with only a certain number of students. (Since selecting students for a support group requires fuller treatment, it's discussed in detail in Chapter 7.)

## Scheduling

Most groups meet once a week. This allows time for individuals to digest the group experience at their own pace and minimizes interference with the students' other classes.

Most support groups meet during the school day, even though this conflicts with class time. After-school transportation would be a problem for many younger students, and some students don't want their parents to know they're in a group, as would be evident if they met after school. Moreover, support groups should be viewed as an integral part of the educational curriculum, not as an after-school exercise. An exception to meeting during school hours would be those students participating in Drug Information Groups as a result of school policy, since these groups are often held after school in lieu of school suspension.

Scheduling support groups to meet at the same time each week is likely to cause problems with the faculty; a rotating schedule solves this problem. One particular day of the week is designated as the group day, and the groups rotate through the available class periods. For example, if there are seven periods in the school schedule and the group rotates through all seven, students would miss any given class only once every seven weeks. Remember, too, that students who miss some classes because of participating in a support group miss far fewer classes than do students with chemical-abuse problems.

Educators should be given a group schedule every month. This way, they're notified in advance when a student will be absent from their classes, and arrangements can be made for homework assignments and examinations that might otherwise be missed. (A sample group schedule is included in Addendum 4.1.)


## Parental Consent

Parental-consent rules deserve careful forethought, especially for students in a Concerned Persons Group. We need to balance several factors: parents' rights to privacy, children's needs, and the school's desire to do what's necessary for students and at the same time avoid any lawsuits.

Generally speaking, the school must obtain parents' consent for grade-school children to participate in a support group. As students become older, though, the issue becomes less clear-cut. For a Recovery Group and a Drug Information Group, it's usually easy to obtain consent because most parents of such students are already concerned about their son's or daughter's chemical abuse.

Parental-consent rules for a Concerned Persons Group aren't as simple. Because of their own denial and fears, some chemically dependent parents wouldn't want their child to be in this sort of group. Knowing this, many students don't want to be in a group if their parents must be notified.

The simplest solution is to mail to the parents of **all** students a letter describing the various groups the school offers. The letter states that if parents don't want their child to participate in a group they should contact the school; otherwise the school will assume it isn't a problem. Besides dealing with the parental-consent issue, the letter also informs the parents what services are available and encourages those who are already concerned about their child to seek out those services. (A sample letter of this sort is given in Addendum 4.3.)

By the time students have entered adolescence, they have a right to exercise at least a modicum of autonomy. There's nothing freakish, exceptional, or wrong about exploring their feelings, practicing communication skills, or learning about chemical dependence.

Don't spend large amounts of time and energy worrying about parental consent or playing the secrecy game. A student doesn't need parental consent to talk with the school counselor, and belonging to a support group is essentially the same thing. Think of support groups as an integral part of the school curriculum, easily accessible to all students, and the groups will become just that.

Occasionally parents will refuse to let their child participate in a support group. If so, first explain the purpose and content of the support group to them, because they're often misinformed about the group. If this approach fails, pair up the student with one of the school counselors for individual counseling sessions so the student can receive help.

## Confidentiality

Students have a right to confidentiality. It's not appropriate or helpful to tell sixty staff members that Jane, a ninth grader, has been abused by her uncle and that her father drinks every day, which leaves her to take care of her brother because her mother left with another man. Obviously, Jane wouldn't want this to be public knowledge, and when she talks with a counselor or in a group about these matters, she assumes they'll be treated confidentially.

But since Jane's teachers have a right to know that she'll be missing their classes, they need at least some information. This information should be given on a need-to-know basis only. A simple method is to assign each group on the monthly schedule a letter of the alphabet. From that point on the group is referred to by letter only; the group letter doesn't signify any particular type of group (see Addendum 4.1). This way, Jane's teachers know she's participating in a group and which classes she'll miss during that month, but they don't know which type of group she's in or what her specific problems are. Some educators, concerned about a student and wanting to help, will ask for additional information. This can be shared when appropriate. For example, a teacher might approach you with concerns about a student in your support group who's not completing assignments and is extremely withdrawn and restless in class. Sharing information about what's happening in the student's personal life, and how the teacher should respond to the student, can be helpful for both the student and the teacher.


## Policies on Physical and Sexual Abuse

Sometimes you'll learn that one of your group members is being physically or sexually abused. The student might reveal this in the group, or you might discover it yourself. Students affected by chemical dependence, especially those with chemically dependent parents, are more often sexually or physically abused than other students. Here are some signs to look for:
- unexplainable or oddly placed bruises;
- fears for, and protection of, younger siblings;

- inappropriate sexual behavior;
- fear of being touched.

If your suspicions are aroused, talk to the student **after** a group meeting about your concerns. Trust your instincts. It never hurts to ask.

If a student brings up the subject during a group meeting, let him or her finish talking and then say you'd like to talk with him or her in more detail about this afterward. A support group isn't an appropriate setting to deal with this issue, but handling it in this way lets the other members know you take the subject seriously and will take action.

Of course, you need a school policy that has a definite procedure to follow: whom you report the abuse to and what steps are to be taken. And you need to be familiar with the abuse policy and procedures **before** the need arises.

Talk with the student long enough to obtain the facts about the abuse. Then connect him or her with the school counselor, social worker, or whoever is supposed to take action in these matters. Don't delay. And don't tell the student he or she should talk to the counselor and leave it at that. Rather, accompany the student to the counselor and sit in on at least the first part of the meeting.

Be careful not to make promises to the student that you won't be able to keep, such as "Don't worry; your father doesn't need to find out." Instead, tell the student, "I'm not sure what will happen, but I know we have to do something." The abuse must be reported, regardless of the student's wishes. **This exception to the group confidentiality rule should be stated to the students during the first session of the group.**


**Closed Group vs. Open Group**

Referrals for support groups won't all come at the same time. Although it would be nice to be able to place students in a group immediately, once a group has started, the new referral must wait for another group to form even if that means waiting until the next semester. Adding a student to a group already in progress can jeopardize the existing level of trust and intimacy, and the new student will miss out on information given in previous sessions.

A Recovery Group is an exception to this rule. When a student returns to school after completing a treatment program, he or she should be assigned to a group right away. This group continues throughout the year; it doesn't have the closed time frame that other groups follow. And since a Recovery Group doesn't have a specific weekly format, there isn't the problem of missed information as there is with the other two support groups. Most importantly, students in recovery need to get into a group right away because of their vulnerability.

## The Group Room

Classrooms aren't ideal group rooms. They're too large, too filled with desks, and seem to elicit the random, often evasive, interaction that students are accustomed to in regular classrooms. A group room should be small in order to create an intimate, secure feeling, and ideally there shouldn't be any windows that can create a visual distraction. The room must also be in an area where outside noise won't intrude. A carpeted floor is helpful for the occasional times when group activities require everyone to be sitting on the floor.

It's worth your while to spend some time looking for a good group room. Physical suroundings and location play an important part in the effectiveness of the group experience.

## Basic Rules for the Group

Most students participating in a support group will be unaccustomed to the boundaries and expectations of a such a group. These boundaries and expectations can be translated into a few basic rules that are discussed during the first session. Here are some guidelines to consider when making rules for your group:

- Have a minimum number of rules. There's no need to make rules covering every unwanted behavior. This is a support group, not a class. Instead of having numerous rules, let group process take care of problem behavior.
- Keep the rules simple. Constructing rules that are simple and clear will ensure that the students understand them.
- Enforce the rules consistently. Follow through with consequences each time a rule is broken, and with every student who breaks one. If you're not prepared to do so, change the rule or discard it.

Type up rules in contract form, and give everyone a copy of the contract during the first session of the group. After discussing the rules and answering any questions, the students should sign their contracts and hand them in to the group leader. This is their pledge to adhere to the rules of the group. (Addendum 4.2 presents sample rules in contract form for the three different types of groups.)

Generally group rules should cover three basic areas:

- **Confidentiality.** The group needs to feel safe so that personal disclosure can take place without fear. A confidentiality rule will encourage this personal sharing.
- **Attendance.** It's important that everyone be present each session and that the leader be made aware of a student's decision to leave the group.
- **Abstinence.** Students need to understand the specific rules for their group regarding abstinence from chemical use.

The fundamental rule for any group is confidentiality. Students won't take risks if they think that what they share in the group will become common knowledge throughout the school or will be relayed to their parents. The rule is this: "Who you see here and what you hear here must stay here." Make sure that the students know that this rule applies to the group leaders also, **but with two exceptions**: Any instances of physical or sexual abuse and any hurting of oneself or others will be reported to the appropriate source. The students need to know this up front. (Actions the group leader should take in these cases were discussed earlier in this chapter.)

If group confidence has been broken, one of the members will no doubt tell you so, most likely in private. Bring this information to the group the following week, and confront the student suspected of breaking the rule. Any student who breaks the group's confidence should be removed. If the members see that you take this rule seriously, they too will take it seriously. You can't compromise on confidentiality.

Another rule that applies to all groups concerns the use of mind-altering chemicals: "Don't come to a group meeting under the influence of any mind-altering chemicals." With a Concerned Persons Group this won't be much of a problem because most students in this type of group aren't abusing chemicals. If they are, they should be placed in a Drug Information Group instead.

Sometimes a student comes to a Drug Information Group under the influence of a mind-altering chemical. Make sure the consequences for breaking this rule are crystal clear. The students need to know in advance that they'll be removed from the group immediately and that school policy will be followed. This policy will most likely include suspension, notification of parents, and, if chemicals are found in their possession, the involvement of the police department. Students who come to a Drug Information Group high or drunk are definitely in serious trouble with their chemical use and should be referred to an agency that can conduct a thorough chemical dependence evaluation. (Referrals such as this are discussed in more depth in Chapter 9.)

Although it would be rare for a student in recovery to come to a group meeting under the influence, there will be occasions when students talk about having used during the previous week. Some of these students are under strict abstinence contracts with parents and with the juvenile court. Don't assume the position of being the only caregiver in this student's life to know that he or she is using chemicals again. Give students the chance to take responsibility for their actions by saying that you think they should share this information with their parents, twelve-step group, and other counselor(s). If students aren't willing to do this, inform them that if they don't do so, you will. Obviously, this policy needs to be clearly stated during the initial session of a group. Confidentiality should protect students' privacy, but not their relapses.

A few other rules might be made specifically for the type of support group and the needs of your particular school and this particular group. These rules might include total abstinence for the duration of the group cycle, or mandatory participation in an aftercare program or twelve-step group for those in a Recovery Group.

*Addendum 4.1*
## Group Schedule

| M | T | W | T | F |
|---|---|---|---|---|
| | | Group Period<br>A   2<br>B   4<br>C   6 | | |
| 1 | 2 | 3 | 4 | 5 |
| | | Group Period<br>A   3<br>B   5<br>C   7 | | |
| 8 | 9 | 10 | 11 | 12 |
| | | Group Period<br>A   4<br>B   6<br>C   8 | | |
| 15 | 16 | 17 | 18 | 19 |
| | | Group Period<br>A   5<br>B   7<br>C   2 | | |
| 22 | 23 | 24 | 25 | 26 |
| | | | | |
| 29 | 30 | | | |

**Note:** Staff members receive this schedule with the names included; students in a group are given the same schedule but without any names.

**Group A**
John Wald
Sally Hanson
Connie Weston
Lee Annmeier
Will Linke

**Group B**
Jerry Muenster
Sheila Sorrell
Dick Schonecker
Mary Suren
Kathy Bolsten
Matt Houger

**Group C**
Camille Clocke
Kris Caraway
Sue Masters
Edith Martens
Glenn Enders
Mort Materns

## Rules for a Concerned Persons Group

- I will not talk with anyone outside of my support group about who is in my group or what other members have shared.
- I will not come to a group meeting under the influence of any mind-altering chemicals.
- If I decide I do not want to continue in this group, I will discuss it with my group leader before I quit.

Signed _____

Date _____

# Rules for a Drug Information Group

- I will not talk with anyone outside of my support group about who is in my group or what other members have shared.
- I will not come to a group meeting under the influence of any mind-altering chemicals.
- If I am participating in this group voluntarily, I will not quit the group without discussing it first with the group leader. If my participation is mandatory, I understand that my attendance will be reported to those involved with my placement in this group.

Signed _____

Date _____

# Rules for a Recovery Group

- I will not talk with anyone outside of my support group about who is in my group or what other members have shared.
- I will not come to a group meeting under the influence of any mind-altering chemicals.
- If I decide I do not want to continue in this group, I will discuss it with my group leader before I quit.
- If I do use any mind-altering chemicals at any other time, I will talk about it in the group the next time we meet.

Signed _____

Date _____

# Letter to Parents

*To all parents:*

Alcohol and other drug use is a problem that students will inevitably be confronted with. Here in our school we want to do our part to equip students to deal with this issue in positive ways. Among the variety of resources available to students are our support groups. Three different types are currently available:

- **Concerned Persons Group.** This support group is for any students who have experienced problems or concerns stemming from someone else's alcohol or other drug use. The group meets weekly for twelve weeks each semester.
- **Drug Information Group.** This support group is for students experiencing problems stemming from their own alcohol or other drug use. The group meets weekly for seven weeks each quarter.
- **Recovery Group.** This support group is for students who have abused alcohol or other drugs but who have either given them up on their own or have completed a chemical dependence treatment program and need assistance in maintaining their sobriety. The group meets weekly throughout the school year.

These groups meet for a single class period once a week. The period in which the support group meets is rotated regularly so that students miss very little time from any one class. Students are required to make up work missed while participating in a support group.

These support groups are a valuable resource for our students and staff, and we want to be able to offer them to any student who wishes to join. If we don't hear otherwise from you, we'll assume it's okay for your son or daughter to participate.

If you have any questions or concerns or would like to discuss involving your son or daughter in one of these groups, please don't hesitate to call our counseling department at _____ . All information will be treated confidentially and respectfully.

Sincerely,

*Chapter 5*

# Building a Support-Group Program

A single successful support group will naturally evolve into additional support groups, more group leaders, and increased community awareness. All of this requires the structure that only a **program** can provide. While so far we've focused on what happens inside a single support group, we now need to discuss the bigger picture, that of an entire support-group program and how to build it.

The ideal support-group program has several components. In the ideal program there are a number of educators who are experienced in leading support groups. Some of them are currently leading a group, while others are ready to get involved if they're needed. All three types of support groups are running concurrently during the school year. A coordinator oversees all support groups, schedules their meetings and meetings for the leaders, and talks with newly referred students. Finally, there's a communication network that allows teachers, administrators, parents, and students to refer students to a support group.

## Evolution of a Typical Support-Group Program

If you're working in a school that's starting its first support group, the task might seem huge. But remember, programs take time to develop. Most of them start with just two motivated educators who are concerned about their students and want to start a support group.

To give you a brief overall look at the structure of a program, here's a fictional example of how a typical program, seen in its broadest outlines, evolves over time.

Two educators who witnessed the effects of chemical dependence on their students and who were troubled by the lack of available resources decided they wanted to organize a support group in their school. They convinced the principal that a group would be a good idea, enlisted the help of the counseling staff, and attended some workshops to learn more about the effects of chemical dependence. Armed with new ideas and some basic group-counseling skills, they designed a group format, met with students referred to them by the school counselor, and set up a schedule in which the group met each week during one of the educators' preparation periods.

In the second year they decided to ask for referrals from other sources. They informed the staff about the type of students appropriate for the support group and made certain that both students and parents were aware of this new service. Soon more students than there was space for wanted to be in the group. The educators decided to split up and have one educator lead a new group by himself. The other used the first group as a resource to train a third educator who had expressed interest. Now in the second year there were three group leaders, two groups, and still more referrals coming in from parents and staff. Because using the educators' preparation periods was very constraining, the administration agreed to place a substitute teacher in the educators' classes during the hour they were absent while leading a group.

Each consecutive year a new educator received group leadership training. In the fourth year one of the original leaders moved into a half-time teaching position, which left the other half of her day for support-group work.

By the middle of the fourth year there were seven educators and one counselor who could lead the five scheduled groups, the PTA was helping fund the program, and the support-group coordinator was making sure everything ran smoothly.

This fictional example of how a typical support-group program evolves has presented only the broad outlines of the program. The rest of this chapter explains in some detail how to go about building such a program in your school. Please note that the steps should be taken in the order presented here.

Keep in mind that building a well-constructed support-group **program** is quite different from leading a support group. At times you might find the process of program building frustrating and painfully slow. Even so, you'll discover that quality support groups and the overwhelming number of students who need them will exert a steady pressure that will eventually convince even the most hesitant of school faculties and administrations that the program is badly needed and can be very effective.

## Obtaining Administration Approval

The first step in implementing a support group is to obtain the support of the administration. Your principal might be eager to try this new idea and might not need any convincing at all, or you might run into resistance. Before meeting with the administration, it would be very helpful to **involve the guidance counselors.** These counselors are your natural allies. Since they're probably overrun with students affected by chemical dependence, they'll welcome this new support-group program.

And since they usually have a close working relationship with the administration, they can easily put in a good word for you. Getting their cooperation is especially crucial if those who want to start the program aren't themselves in the counseling department.

Your indispensable personal preparation for getting administration approval is to be very clear in your own mind and to be able to explain these basic issues: the extent of the problem you want to confront, precisely what you want to do, and the benefits to be derived.

• **Understand the extent of the problem.** Do you really know how many students in your school are affected by chemical dependence? Calling the problem "really bad" will hardly convince administrators who don't view the problem as you do. **Get the facts.** First, you can find out the number of students affected by a parent's chemical dependence by consulting a variety of national surveys. A well-accepted statistic to use is that one out of four students is so affected.* Second, an area mental health center, university, or government agency might well have conducted a survey on the use of chemicals among adolescents in your geographical area. If not, consider doing an anonymous survey in your own school. (You can use the sample survey in the Addendum.) It will identify the number of students using mind-altering chemicals. Third, the number of students who have completed a treatment program—and who are therefore chemically dependent and in need of a Recovery Group—can be found by asking the counseling department.

• **Be clear on what you want to do.** How many support groups, and which of the three types, do you want to start? It's always a good idea to start a pilot project like this with a single

---

* See the article "Innocent Bystanders at Risk: The Children of Alcoholics" by Claudia Black, referred to in Chapter 1.

group. If you're anticipating resistance from the administration, you might consider starting with a Drug Information Group. This group addresses a need that almost everyone understands and deems important because students abusing chemicals are visible and are often causing problems in the school.

Also outline beforehand how many hours per week will be involved in organizing and leading the support group, how many students you'll have in each group (discussed in Chapter 4), and where you'll get them (discussed in Chapter 7).

• **Describe the benefits.** Promote the groups by describing how they'll benefit students, staff, and therefore the whole school.

Concerned Persons Group benefits: These students will feel better about themselves, perform better in school, and be less likely to abuse chemicals in years to come.

Drug Information Group benefits: This group will not only provide information about chemical dependence, but will provide constructive confrontation and intervention directed at students' chemical abuse and related behaviors. Moreover, it will give the counselors working with these types of students a third alternative other than an outside referral or suspension. Instead of suspension, it will provide a constructive consequence for the school's alcohol and other drug policy.

Recovery Group benefits: Students returning from a treatment program are much more likely to maintain their sobriety in such a group. This will decrease the need for additional treatment and will result in improved grades, attendance, and attitude.

Staff benefits: In general, students involved in support groups will experience improvements in self-concept, attitudes, and overall mental health. This naturally translates into better attendance, attitudes, and grades. It also improves educators' morale because they now have effective tools with which to help students who are struggling with the effects of chemical dependence.

## Appointing a Support-Group Coordinator

When your school is starting its first support group, most likely two motivated educators will constitute the entire program: They'll gather the referrals, coordinate schedules, and lead the support group. But when a school system already has a few groups in place, it becomes important to have a coordinator— a person responsible for overseeing the whole support-group program. This person contacts newly referred students; develops a group schedule that details how many groups there will be, when they'll meet, who will be in them, and who leads them; coordinates the training of new group leaders; and schedules monthly meetings for the entire support-group program staff.

The coordinator can be an educator, school counselor, Student Assistance Program director, or a staff member hired specifically for this job. If the person is an educator, he or she should be freed of part of his or her normal teaching responsibilities if possible, because it can be difficult to teach full time and effectively coordinate a support-group program.

## Involving Other Educators

It's important not to ignore other educators in your school. Training staff members in group leadership skills will allow you to help more students affected by chemical dependence. Besides being available to co-lead groups, these leaders will become key support people who will emphasize the attributes of the groups to other educators in staff lounges and during planning meetings. When an occasional faculty member complains about a student missing class because of belonging to a group, these people will be the program's allies.

A pool of trained educators will also help ensure the program's longevity. As leaders' interests and energies wax and wane, so do the groups. If there are only two support-group leaders and they lose interest or leave the school system, the groups could vanish. Training a number of additional educators will help ensure that there will always be groups available for students who need them.

### Involving the Community

Support groups don't exist in a vacuum. Besides the administration and the staff, there's the larger community beyond the school walls. In this community are parents concerned about their children, mental health professionals looking for resources for their clients, volunteer organizations looking for worthwhile projects. Establishing ties with that larger community as well as with all the people in your own school helps ensure continued support and financing of the support-group program. Consider in particular these points about involving both the whole school and the larger community.

• **Win over your opposition.** Opposition to groups often stems from fear and misinformation. If misinformed people can be shown what happens in support groups and how helpful these groups are to students, they'll most likely become allies. Let them inspect the group's program and talk to student members who are willing to discuss how the group has benefited them. After making certain that it won't disrupt the group, invite a key opponent to participate in a support group. This person can attend each session in the same way that an apprentice group leader would. This can be an excellent way to transform skeptical or opposed persons, including administrators, into program allies.

• **Publicize success.** When parents of a group member tell you how grateful they are that these groups are available, encourage them to tell the school administration. Publicize the support groups in the school newsletter and at PTA meetings so as to make sure the community is aware of the group program and its effectiveness. Ask your local newspaper if it would consider interviewing the support group leaders about the program.

• **Network with area chemical dependence professionals.** Many counselors will be grateful to have these groups available as a referral resource. Once this relationship is established, the support groups can't disappear from the school without a fight from these community counselors. Encourage relationships with the professionals by visiting their offices and requesting referrals. Perhaps the most effective way to build a relationship with them is to refer students from your support groups to their agency. They'll reciprocate.

• **Invite community participation.** Many community groups are looking for good causes to work with, especially in the area of drug prevention. Don't be an island; let them help. They can help raise funds to assist the support groups, can publicize the program, and can co-lead groups. Involving them broadens your base of support and helps ensure the program's permanence in the school system.


## Choosing Group Leaders

It's important to choose group leaders carefully. For example, Bill, an English teacher, has a son who has gone through treatment, so Bill understands chemical dependence well, yet he comes across to his students as somewhat angry and threatening. So students wouldn't talk about feelings if he were leading the group. And then there's Susan, who teaches art. She's warm and approachable, but is uncomfortable with conflict. If Susan were in charge of a support group, students wouldn't be challenged to make any changes. For Bill and Susan, having some appropriate characteristics for group leadership doesn't make up for their basic weaknesses.

Many factors influence the selection process, and of course some are more important than others. The following list of qualities will help you choose the **best** potential group leaders. Keep in mind, of course, that we're describing ideal group leaders. Don't expect to find perfection at this early stage. Questions are listed after each of these qualities. Apply them to each candidate during the selection process.

• **Commitment:** A group leader should have a deep and demonstrated commitment to helping confused, hurting students, not just a stated interest.

— Does this person regularly show care and concern for students? Young adults can sense whether someone's caring is genuine.

— When the support group gets rough or is no longer interesting for its novelty, will the novice group leader see it through? After investing your training energy and time, you'll want your leader to be around awhile. One year for training and at least two years of service are reasonable expectations. Don't choose educators who aren't planning to work in your school for at least three years.

• **Relationship Skills:** Building trusting relationships with clients is the key to effective counseling. Research indicates that the strongest factor in effecting a positive change in a client isn't the precise counseling technique or even the caregiver's theoretical perspective, but the quality of the relationship.

It's especially important that new support-group leaders have the ability to develop challenging yet supportive relationships with the students in their groups. This is a rather difficult quality to define, but you know it when you see it. Students talk about these educators in affectionate terms, say hello to them in the halls, and spend time in their classes after school. They command respect from the students instead of demanding it, but they know how to work on the student's level. They're dynamic, energetic, and fair, and the students truly trust them.

— Does the person have a favorable reputation with students?

— Do staff members like the person?

— Do students approach the person with problems, school-related or otherwise?

— Is the person direct and honest?

• **Intrapersonal Awareness:** Since group leaders will be helping students through some difficult personal struggles, a potential support-group leader should also have experienced some personal difficulties and found the resources to work through them.

— Is the person at ease with himself/herself and others?

— Is the person comfortable talking about his/her own emotions?

— Did past events result in personal struggles and growth that would give this person insight into the lives of support-group members?

— Can the person explain the dynamics of shame, loneliness, anger, and grief, citing examples of when he/she has experienced the same feelings?

If your candidate can't stand up to these questions, it's best not to use him or her. This person won't have much to offer students who are attempting to understand and work through these types of difficult feelings.

• **Personal Issues That May Interfere:** Some educators who express a desire to become group leaders have personal problems of such magnitude that they would seriously interfere with their being able to lead a support group effectively. Obviously, an educator who abuses chemicals would be a poor choice for a group leader. Again, a support-group leader who has a chemically dependent spouse or child may be a less obvious but equally important concern. You'll want to make certain that he or she has come to some sort of resolution of this problem. If so, and if the person meets the other criteria, he or she can still make an excellent leader.

— Does the person have a reputation of being a heavy drinker or user of other drugs?

— Is there chemical dependence in another family member? If so, what has the potential leader done about it?

• **Group Skills:** While many specific leadership skills will be gained through experience, some expertise in communication dynamics and effective teaching skills are prerequisites.

— Does the person look you in the eye when he/she communicates?

— Does the person demonstrate the ability to handle conflict effectively?

— Do peers acknowledge the person to be an effective educator?

• **Knowledge of Chemical Dependence:** Group leaders will eventually need an understanding of the dynamics of chemical use, abuse, and dependence. They'll need to become familiar with the process of treatment and the various twelve-step groups. If a new group leader doesn't already have this knowledge, he or she must be willing to acquire it during training. Any practical, experiential knowledge is a real plus here. Such knowledge would be characteristic of educators who are in recovery from chemical dependence, are members of a twelve-step group, or have a chemically dependent family member.

— Has the person completed any coursework in chemical dependence?

— Is the person "streetwise" about chemicals and adolescents?

— Is the person familiar with twelve-step programs?

— Does the person have any personal experience with chemical dependence in his/her family or close friends?

Although actually choosing from the list of educators who would like to be group leaders might be difficult, finding volunteers is relatively easy. Spread the word in the faculty lounge and at staff meetings through anouncements, posters, and word-of-mouth. If an educator who you think would make an excellent group leader doesn't volunteer, ask the person yourself.

There are sources other than just your school staff for potential leaders. After being screened for possible problems and given some training, pastors, volunteers from mental health organizations, PTA members, or members of a twelve-step group could become excellent volunteer group leaders. If you're having difficulty finding interested staff members, solicit help from the larger community. These volunteer leaders will help ensure effective group experiences for the students and will increase community support and networking without burdening the school's finances.

To avoid hurt feelings and suspicions of elitism, interview every staff member who expresses an interest in becoming a group leader. Everyone deserves a chance. Fortunately, educators who express their interest will usually have at least some of the qualities the position demands. Those who aren't chosen should be told why in a straightforward but courteous way.

After all candidates have been interviewed, the program coordinator, school counselors, administration, and group leaders, or a combination of all these must make the final choice. Make certain that staff members who understand the group process and have the requisite skills are present for the interviews and the decision-making process.

Although this entire process can be difficult and time-consuming, it's a challenge that must be met. A group with a leader who isn't comfortable talking about feelings, for example, will be a group that doesn't talk about feelings. Or a group with a leader who's afraid of conflict will be a group where no one is challenged to change.


### Training Group Leaders

Learning the practical aspects of leading support groups involves three basic phases: the observation phase, the apprenticeship phase, and the co-leadership phase. During the first two phases, the aspiring leader is paired up with an experienced group leader. These two educators co-lead the group. The senior leader is responsible for providing the appropriate training experience—e.g., answering questions and giving performance feedback to the apprentice leader. Since most groups take the larger part of a semester, the first two phases of training will last one school year.

Providing the training experience in phases allows both the senior leader and the apprentice leader to stop and reevaluate performance at the end of each group cycle. Sometimes apprentice leaders don't realize exactly what they're getting into, and these review points will give them permission to back out if they so choose. They also provide an opportunity for the senior trainer to tactfully eliminate potential group leaders who aren't working out as anticipated. At the end of each training phase there should be a meeting between the senior trainer, the apprentice leader, and the support-group program coordinator. At these meetings you can discuss performance, problems, and whether all three parties think the training should continue.

• **Phase One—Observation:** This initial phase of training is designed to familiarize the apprentice leader with group process and the format. The apprentice isn't a leader here; instead, he or she participates in the group just as a student would. By taking part in all activities, the educator sees the group through the eyes of a student.

Before the training starts, be certain that all expectations are discussed. The apprentice in training should:

— participate in group as a member, not as a leader;

— take notes on activities and group process;

— follow all rules, including group confidentiality and regular attendance;

— make time for discussion after each group session.

Give the new leader a group format guide that includes a general outline of the group sessions and a listing of the goals and activities for each session (see Addendum 8.1). This way, the trainee will be able to follow the process closely and with understanding.

Encourage the apprentice to take notes and to ask questions after each group session. It's important to have regular meetings with the apprentice; the best time is immediately after each session of a group. Usually the apprentice will have questions such as "Why did you do that during the session?" or "How come Mark acts that way whenever you ask him a question?" After educators' initial exposure to the personal problems that the students discuss in a group, it's common for them to express some sadness and anger, making comments like "I just had no idea that this was going on in their homes."

• **Phase Two—Apprenticeship:** The apprentice becomes a co-leader in this phase. For one complete cycle of the group, he or she has the opportunity to practice leading group activities that were introduced during the first phase of training. All this takes place with the support of the senior group leader. The co-leaders can switch off every week, alternating being responsible for each session, or they can split up the sessions into two parts, each taking half. Regardless of how the responsibilities are shared, this phase of the training encourages preliminary experience in group leadership and provides the apprentice with opportunities for discussion and feedback with the senior group leader.

• **Phase Three—Co-leadership:** With the previous two phases of training successfully completed, the apprentice has participated in two separate groups. Most likely this has required the major part of a school year. In the third phase the apprentice is assigned a new group and a co-leader, preferably someone other than his or her trainer of the previous year so that the apprentice is exposed to different leadership styles. It's absolutely essential that the apprentice have a co-leader for support during this third phase. Being responsible for a group can be difficult for some at first, and the apprentice will frequently need help, encouragement, and someone who can come to the rescue when major problems arise. As in all groups, the co-leaders should schedule regular meetings to discuss their group and its progress and problems.

### Providing Support for Group Leaders

New leaders will still need support and advice while they're working with their own support groups. Even the most experienced leaders need to meet regularly to discuss problems, progress, and other issues. There may well be occasions when a leader will have a troublesome student in a group, or when the support group isn't going anywhere and the leader is feeling stuck. Suggestions from experienced peers can be very helpful in such cases.

These meetings also provide opportunities to share personal problems. Working with students affected by chemical dependence can be emotionally demanding, and some leaders may overextend themselves to the point where they actually begin to feel that they're responsible for solving the students' problems. These meetings will encourage an awareness of this danger and will foster growth in such skills as detachment and self-preservation. They can also be a forum for discussing new group activities and new format ideas, and for communicating scheduling information. Many schools schedule group-leader meetings monthly, before or after school. However your school accomplishes it, make sure that group leaders aren't simply assigned groups and left on their own.

## Deciding on the Number of Leaders in a Group

The number of leaders in each group is worth careful consideration. While theoretically there could be twice as many groups operating if each had only one leader, leading groups alone can be a problem. Even though an experienced group leader can handle almost anything that comes up in the group, there are times when a co-leader can be invaluable. We all have our shortcomings and blind spots, and chances are that one co-leader's strengths will make up for another's weaknesses. During group sessions co-leaders often come to each other's rescue and then afterward discuss what happened, giving each other helpful feedback and suggestions.

Unfortunately, because of limited resources, two leaders might not always be available for each group. Even though it's possible to lead a group by yourself once you have considerable experience, **it's best that apprentice and beginning group leaders have a co-leader**. This is not only for the students' sake but for the leaders' sake as well. There are often so many things going on during a group session—concepts you're trying to get across, a student exhibiting unmanagable behavior—that you'll welcome the help.

## Finding Time to Lead Support Groups

Most schools provide a substitute teacher for the class period that the group leader will miss. Since educators typically lead only one group, they're absent from just one class period per week. Similar arrangements are made for educators in training. If a school is so financially strapped that the administration objects to this, it's still possible to free up time for group leaders. Groups can be scheduled during the group leaders' free period, or a system can be arranged wherein other educators volunteer to take over the group leader's class during their own free periods. Obviously, this will take place only when there are motivated staff members who are willing to help. And even when teachers are willing to volunteer their time, this sort of approach should be seen as only a temporary measure, while the groups are proving their effectiveness to a doubting administration. Any worthwhile effort to provide support groups to students requires a financial commitment from the administration and a policy that provides for employing substitute teachers.

# Survey of Chemical Use

This is a survey to learn how many students are using chemicals. The term "chemicals" refers to any drug, including alcohol. **Don't put your name on this survey!** After the information is taken from the sheets, the sheets will be discarded. **No one will know your identity**, so please be honest.

Indicate how often you have used these chemicals:

| | Never | 1-3 Times | Once a Month or Less | Up to Twice a Week | Twice a Week or More |
|---|---|---|---|---|---|
| 1. Alcohol (beer, wine, liquor) | A | B | C | D | E |
| 2. Marijuana (hash, hash oil, THC) | A | B | C | D | E |
| 3. Inhalants (rush, gasoline, glue) | A | B | C | D | E |
| 4. Pills (uppers, downers, speed) | A | B | C | D | E |
| 5. Hallucinogens (mushrooms, LSD) | A | B | C | D | E |
| 6. Cocaine (crack, rock) | A | B | C | D | E |
| 7. PCP (angel dust) | A | B | C | D | E |
| 8. Narcotics (heroin, codeine, opium) | A | B | C | D | E |

9. How old are you?

A
10-11

B
12-13

C
14-15

D
16-17

E
18-19

10. What is your gender?

A
male

B
female

11. What percentage of your friends use alcohol or other drugs?

A
0-20%

B
21-40%

C
41-60%

D
61-80%

E
81-100%

12. How serious do you consider the problem of chemical abuse among students in this school?

A
I don't know.

B
I don't think there is a problem.

C
There is a very small problem.

D
There is a problem for a minority of students.

E
It is a very serious problem that affects a majority of students.

*Chapter 6*

# Strengths Needed in a Group Leader

The strengths discussed in this chapter are indispensable to you as a support-group leader, and they play a vital role in the success of your group and of the whole program. These strengths will help you become a knowledgeable and caring adult who can make a significant contribution to confused and hurting students. It's encouraging to know, too, that these strengths will grow and deepen right along with your experience in leading groups.

### Knowing Your Community Resources

Many students are referred to support groups by **area mental health agencies.** Since some students will be referred back to those same community resources for counseling when your support group ends, becoming familiar with the various counseling and treatment services in your community is important.

**Twelve-step programs** are another important resource to know about. You should certainly be familiar with such outstanding groups as Alcoholics Anonymous (A.A.), Narcotics Anonymous (N.A.), Al-Anon, Alateen, and Adult Children of

Alcoholics meetings (see the list of national organizations in Resources). Talking to program members, attending open meetings, and reading the free literature available at these meetings will help you understand what these excellent self-help programs have to offer your students. Closed twelve-step meetings are only for members and for newcomers who wish to protect their anonymity; open meetings are for everyone. Be aware that not all meetings are the same. Twelve-step groups seem to have personalities just as people do, so attend several different meetings.

Understanding twelve-step programs is important for a variety of reasons. Many of the students participating in a support group will either be involved in these programs themselves or will have a family member who is. These self-help groups are the most popular and effective ongoing support systems for people after their treatment program or therapy is terminated. Here are just a few examples of issues related to twelve-step programs that will be raised in a support group:

- A student in your Concerned Persons Group is worried about her father and his faltering A.A. attendance.
- A student in your Drug Information Group is complaining because she's being forced to go to N.A. meetings. She doesn't want to go and has no idea of what to expect.
- A student in your school just started participating in a Recovery Group and wants to know where and when A.A. meetings are held.

You can be sure such questions will be asked. If you've attended several meetings, you'll be better able to answer such questions and provide the encouragement students need.


**Improving Your Group Skills
and Knowledge of Chemical Dependence**

Participating in workshops on topics related to chemical

dependence and to the skills needed in support groups will give you new information and ideas, teach you new techniques, and help you gain insights about yourself. These workshops can range from one-day presentations consisting mostly of conceptual material, to a week-long training program where you'll be able to participate in actual sessions of a support group.

To learn about workshops offered locally, check with area colleges, universities, treatment centers, or your state alcohol and other drug commission. The Johnson Institute in Minneapolis offers a wide variety of professional training seminars on chemical dependence-related issues plus seminars dealing specifically with young people and their problems with chemicals. Furthermore, the Resources given at the end of this book list the names and addresses of many national organizations and suggest a rich variety of other sources of information and ideas: books, workbooks, booklets, periodicals, films, and videocassettes.

### Resolving Behavior Problems in a Group

Your groups will usually run smoothly—but not always. Encountering behavior problems doesn't necessarily mean that you're an ineffective group leader. Some students who exhibit dysfunctional behavior are experiencing problems of their own or their families' making, and they may act out these problems through negative attitudes and innappropriate behavior.

What do you do when a group member is angry and hostile or distant and uncommunicative? How should you handle students who chat off to the side while you're presenting an important concept? Here are two simple guidelines to follow in these and similar situations:

**Guideline 1: Confront the problem.** "Bob, I'm aware that whenever we talk about sad or painful feelings you appear to start joking or clowning." "Cindy, I'm wondering why it is that although everyone else in the group attempts to share, you don't seem to have anything to say." By doing this you're directing the problem back to its source. If the problem evokes strong feelings in you, it can be even more effective to report those feelings while you're confronting a group member. For instance: "You know, Jim and Sue, I'm feeling frustrated because I'm trying to talk about the Alateen program and you two are carrying on your own conversation. I get the impression that you aren't interested in what I have to say." "Kris, I'm feeling hurt right now because it appears you're making fun of me behind my back."

These students are accustomed to adults' being authoritative, saying things like "If you don't quit, I'm going to. . ." or "Listen here, young lady. . ." Such statements are provocative and are sure to escalate the problem. Instead, focus directly on the issue, address the student(s) by name, use direct eye contact, and state how you feel. Practice using this type of sentence structure: "I feel_____ when you_____."

**Guideline 2: Direct the problem back to the group.** There will be occasional conflict in your group. For example, the members might disagree on what topic to talk about at the meeting, or one student might accuse another of being dishonest, or you might sense underlying hostility in the group. Don't automatically assume responsibility for the problem. This is the group's problem, not yours. It's an opportunity for students to develop their problem-solving skills—as long as you don't jump in and take control. Call attention to the problem (Guideline 1) and then ask, "So what are **we** going to do about this? Does anyone have any suggestions?" List alternatives, discuss the problem and/or vote on it, but resist the urge to fix it. Conflict isn't necessarily bad; it's a positive sign that your group is working, because conflict arises naturally in intimate group settings. If there's never any conflict in your group, it probably means that the members are afraid of taking risks by sharing their thoughts or feelings or of investing themselves in the group.*

## Being Compassionate

The most important quality that anyone who works in the counseling profession can possess is a true desire to help those in need. Behind the variety of sophisticated techniques for delivering effective services is a genuine caring and empathy for others. It really is as simple, and as powerful, as that.

When this point is forgotten, one can get lost in the complexities of program development. The groups can become streamlined but also empty and ineffective when the focus is on technique instead of on the problems of the students. Certainly, much of your energy should be put into developing skills and programs. But don't forget that compassion—demonstrated by your understanding, challenging, and supporting group members—is the key to healing. As your experience with the group grows and the students and their problems tend to blur together, be mindful of your main focus: your group members.

## Clearing Up Your Personal Problems

Being human, group leaders can sometimes bring to a group personal problems that are detrimental to the group. We never leave ourselves at the door of the group room. Many chemical dependence counselors are themselves in recovery from chemical dependence or are adult children of chemically dependent parents. This may or may not make them better counselors. You

---

* To learn more about group conflict, consult pages 225-267 in *From Peer Pressure to Peer Support* by Shelley MacKay Freeman. (See Resources.)

don't have to have "been there" to work with people who "are there"—but sometimes it helps. It all depends on what you've done with your own personal problems. If you've worked through them, this will be a strength you can offer others. If you're still among the "walking wounded," get your personal life in order **before** you start trying to bring healing to others.

You go about this in the same way you'd advise your students to do: Work with a counselor and participate in a support group or in one of the twelve-step self-help programs. Is it appropriate—not to mention fair—for you to expect a student to stop abusing chemicals if you have a drinking problem? Or if you haven't dealt with feelings stemming from a parent's, sibling's, or spouse's chemical dependence, do you think you'll be successful leading a group that's trying to do that very thing? The litmus test is this: Are your personal problems stepping stones to growth, or are they boulders that block your path?

### Establishing and Maintaining Leader/Student Boundaries

Apprentice group leaders will often become personally emmeshed in their group members' lives. It takes time and experience to establish appropriate boundaries between you and your students. These boundaries indicate a recognition that you're a separate person from the students you work with. You can point the way, but they must do the walking.

Many group leaders have an innate sense of these boundaries; other group leaders have to learn them by experience. Ironically, the more caring and sensitive a group leader is, the more likely he or she is to blur these boundaries. Make sure that apprentice group leaders have an opportunity to talk about their support groups and their feelings. It will help them learn about appropriate boundaries.

Students don't need your sympathy; they need your empathy, listening skills, maturity, and suggestions for constructive alternatives to their counterproductive attitudes and behavior. You do the students in your group a disservice when you try to take their hardships from them. Working through their own problems is part of their maturation process. Besides, acting as if you can solve their problems is dishonest; it really isn't possible. You're not God or Super-counselor. Your role in the group is to help students help themselves.

Besides your own limitations, there are limitations to what the groups can do. These groups are for support, not therapy. They won't be able to help everyone, nor will every student affected by chemical dependence even have the opportunity to join a group. It's unfortunate but true. Work hard with the students in your group, give them the best you have to offer, and let go of the rest.

So how do you develop this tough skin and walk the fine line between supporting students and rescuing them from their problems? The answer lies in talking with other group leaders in your school about what's going on inside you and your group. All group leaders must be encouraged to speak up when they think another leader is getting out of balance. This feedback will help leaders keep each other on the right track. Through dialogue with others, listening to yourself, and being aware of your own feelings, you'll learn to recognize the subtle difference between supporting and rescuing.

## Having a Personal Support System

Being a group leader is hard work. Leading groups is very rewarding, but it can also be emotionally draining. You'll witness the suffering and emotional pain of confused, hurting, angry students, some of whom come from hurting, dysfunctional families. Since you're human, this can eventually wear you down.

It's of utmost importance that you take care of **your own** emotional needs. You need to be nurtured by others just as truly as students do. The well within will run dry unless you replenish it. Many support-group leaders do replenish it by attending open Al-Anon meetings regularly where they learn how to be responsible **to** others (their students) instead of being responsible **for** them. Getting your needs met through your students isn't the way to do it. So make certain you have a personal support system of friends, family, and co-workers who will give you what you need. After all, this is what you're teaching your students in the group.

*Chapter 7*

# Finding Students for a Support Group

In Chapter 4, I discussed the steps to take in starting an initial support group in a school. However, in the interest of streamlining that chapter I deliberately bypassed an important issue because it demands somewhat fuller treatment: the issue of finding students for a support group. Now is the time to explore that problem.

The problem is rather difficult because few students affected by chemical dependence will tug at your shirt sleeve and volunteer to be in such a group. Students affected by someone else's chemical dependence (typically a parent's) will, until helped, faithfully keep the family secret by obeying the "no-tell rule." Students who are themselves abusing chemicals often don't want to quit or don't even know they have a problem. Students in our third category, those in recovery, are more likely to seek out a support group, because by now they're motivated to do so and have been instructed by their treatment counselors to do so. But even these students won't approach you unless they know that such a group exists in your school.

## Publicity

Your first step, then, in finding candidates for a support group is to use publicity to make the student body aware that groups are available. Put articles in the school newspaper; make posters; make announcements in homerooms and in classroom presentations.

Still, the dynamics of denial and shame will prevent many students who need a group the most from offering to get involved. So the most productive method for finding new group members is to identify appropriate students and ask them personally to join a group.

## Building a Referral Network

But how do you identify those students? The answer lies primarily in building a referral network. This referral network can be part of an existing Student Assistance Program, can result from a clear school policy for dealing with alcohol and other drug violations, or can simply be the result of cooperation among staff members. By soliciting the help of **staff members** you can identify many students who are affected by chemical dependence. In order to get referrals from staff members, they need to know what type of students you want, how to identify them, and how to refer them to a support group. You can give them this information through staff inservices.

**Parents** and **individual professionals in the community** should also be part of the referral network. Some parents will want their son or daughter to join a support group if they know that such groups are available. (See Parental Consent in Chapter 4 and Addendum 4.3.) **Mental health agencies and treatment centers** will also refer their clients to your groups.

A final referral source is the student's **peers**. If students know about the program and see its merits, they'll be less hesitant to approach a teacher or school counselor about a fellow student's problem. This type of referral will happen more often as the groups establish a positive track record and are viewed positively by the student body.

Even when the network is working well, each of the three types of chemical dependence support groups has its own patterns of referral.

A **Concerned Persons Group** receives few outside referrals. Since most families of these students are in denial, the parents don't often seek help for their children, and most students of this sort won't refer themselves to a support group either.

Further complicating matters is the fact that educators usually aren't aware that they have a student in their class who has a chemically dependent parent. This shouldn't be a surprise: Most of these students are hesitant to reveal this information, and what little signs the educators can notice don't readily identify students as having chemically dependent parents. Poor school performance or preoccupation, for example, could have many causes other than parental chemical dependence.

Since children with chemically dependent parents won't come to you, the support group coordinator and group leaders must go out and find them. One effective method involves organizing a presentation for the health class (or other appropriate class) of the effects of chemical dependence on family members. Two excellent films to use for this purpose are *Different Like Me* and *Soft Is the Heart of a Child*. (See Resources.)

While the information in this presentation is beneficial for all students, the main purpose is to convince students in the class who have a chemically dependent parent that they should get some help for themselves. Even when they understand this, though, most of these students still won't volunteer to be in a Concerned Persons Group, so they must be asked individually. Part of your presentation should include a brief questionnaire that **every** student completes and hands in to you. The students should be told that all the information on the questionnaire will remain confidential. They should also be informed that some students might be approached individually later and invited to join a support group, but that it will be up to the students to decide whether they want to participate in such a group.

The student scores on the questionnaires will identify those students you should invite to join a Concerned Persons Group. (For a questionnaire you can use for this purpose, see Addendum 7.)

After the presentation, put all the questionnaires that have more than a few "yes" responses into one pile. These are the students who should be interviewed individually for a Concerned Persons Group, since there's a good chance that they have a chemically dependent family member. Sometimes, of course, a student won't be appropriate for a Concerned Persons Group, and sometimes a student should be in group but isn't willing to get involved. Still, this method is very productive, and you should be prepared for a large number of students wanting to be in a Concerned Persons Group.

Please make sure your school will have the resources necessary to help these students once you blow the horn offering hope and help. It would be rather unfortunate to tell affected students they need to get some help and then not be able to provide it when they ask.

Typically, referrals to a **Drug Information Group** are initiated by the school administration because of a policy violation, or by a concerned teacher or parent. There aren't many self-referrals to this group, although some younger students who are abusing chemicals will consider a Drug Information Group a novel experience and will join on being asked.

Students appropriate for a **Recovery Group** are the easiest to identify. Most often, they'll refer themselves. But if they don't, the school administration and the counseling department will be aware of a student's return from a treatment center and will usually make the referral if the student doesn't.

## Membership Criteria

Since each of the support groups is designed to meet the needs of a certain type of student, it's important to establish membership guidelines that clearly outline the kinds of students who are appropriate for each type of group. It wouldn't make any sense to include a student in a Concerned Persons Group, for example, unless she has a family member who abuses chemicals. While it might not be harmful to the student, it would affect group cohesion because the other students would identify that student as an outsider. And for the sake of the student you wouldn't want to place someone who doesn't use any chemicals in a Drug Information Group because it would encourage social interaction with students who might well be abusing chemicals regularly. Membership criteria protect both the individual and the group.

Two general rules apply to all three kinds of groups.

**Rule 1: Those students most in need are given the first opportunities to be in a group.** There will be occasions when you simply don't have slots available for all the students who need them. Here, prioritizing is the best solution. Invite the students most in need of a support group to participate. For example, a student with an abusive, chemically dependent mother has a greater need to be in a support group than would a student whose chemically dependent father has been in recovery since the student was four years old.

**Rule 2: The welfare of the group takes precedence over the potential needs of any one student.** There will be instances when one student repeatedly disrupts a group and no amount of problem solving seems to help. Remove such a person from the group, refer him or her to another resource such as a school counselor, and concentrate on the ones who are willing to work. You can't fix everyone.

Although those two guidelines do apply to all three kinds of groups, each group also has its own membership criteria.

Membership criteria for a **Concerned Persons Group** can be somewhat difficult to define. A student could be adversely affected by the chemical dependence of a number of people—parents, siblings, or other relatives. Generally, the closer the ties between the student and the person who's chemically dependent, the more harmful the effects on the student will be.

There are exceptions. There will be cases in which the father is chemically dependent but the student hasn't seen him in ten years. Or a student may be having a difficult time because of her favorite aunt's drinking. Each case will be different, so avoid making assumptions. Instead, ask the students questions about their frustrations and problems related to the people in their lives who abuse chemicals. If you think they're adversely affected by someone else's chemical abuse, ask them if they'd like to be in a Concerned Persons Group. If you don't know whether they've been significantly affected, ask them if they want to be in a group and let them decide.

A **Drug Information Group** has fairly simple guidelines. A student can participate in this group if he or she has a problem with chemical use. While it's more enjoyable to have students who want to be there, it's not a necessity. Many of these students will be in the group because of external pressure. And that's fine. Even if they don't want to be in the group, they'll still learn some things about themselves and their chemical use.

A **Recovery Group** is available to students who have experienced problems with their chemical use but are currently remaining sober. This includes those returning from a treatment center, those who have completed a Drug Information Group and want to remain abstinent, and any other students who have stopped using chemicals and need the support that a Recovery Group can offer.

80

Ideally, all students in a Recovery Group should want to be there, but sometimes this isn't the case. There will be students returning from a treatment center who want to start abusing chemicals again or who don't think they need to be involved in such a group—that they can do it on their own.

A well-functioning Recovery Group will deal with these types of students as they appear. New group members who at first wanted to isolate themselves will start to open up and build relationships with other adolescents in recovery, and the students intent on using will be found out and referred to a counselor or treatment center.

Some students meet the criteria for belonging to more than one kind of support group. As a general rule, if a student is abusing chemicals, confronting this problem must take place first. For example, students who themselves are abusing chemicals and who also have chemically dependent parents will need to deal with their own addiction first, then work on issues related to parental chemical dependence. It's not likely that students can deal successfully with the impact their chemically dependent parents have had on them while they themselves are abusing chemicals.

# Confidential Questionnaire

This report will remain confidential. None of this information will be shared with anyone else without your permission, so please answer the questions honestly. The word "chemical" refers to alcohol and other drugs.

Name _____

Grade _____    Date _____

Please check yes or no to the following questions.

|  | Yes | No |
|---|---|---|
| 1. Are you concerned about a parent's, relative's, or close friend's chemical use? | ☐ | ☐ |
| 2. Do you spend a lot of time thinking about this person's chemical use? | ☐ | ☐ |
| 3. Have you ever thought that this person has a problem with his or her chemical use? | ☐ | ☐ |
| 4. Do you stay out of the house as much as possible because of this person's chemical use? | ☐ | ☐ |
| 5. Are you afraid to upset this person because it may cause him or her to use more chemicals? | ☐ | ☐ |
| 6. Do you feel that no one at home really loves you or cares what happens to you? | ☐ | ☐ |

|  | Yes | No |
|---|---|---|
| 7. Are you afraid or embarrassed to bring your friends home because of a family member's chemical use? | ☐ | ☐ |
| 8. Do you tell lies to cover up for this person's chemical use? | ☐ | ☐ |
| 9. Have you ever wanted to talk to someone about this person's chemical use? | ☐ | ☐ |
| 10. Is your schoolwork suffering because of this person's chemical use? | ☐ | ☐ |

*Chapter 8*

# Format for Each Kind of Support Group

This chapter provides a week-by-week description of what takes place in support-group sessions and gives you, the group leader, instructions on how to conduct those sessions. Study the information provided for the kind of group you'll be leading so you'll understand the goals of each session and can confidently present the materials and lead the activities. (The term "activities" refers to any group procedure such as having a discussion, completing worksheets, viewing a film, or reading from a book.) But first, here are some preliminary suggestions and comments applicable to all three kinds of groups.

It's helpful to keep a group leader's notebook with a separate page outlining each week's session. This way, you can prepare for your group session by reviewing its goals and activities. Addendum 8.1 is a guide for outlining each group session.

The formats for these three support groups are the result of much experimentation with various session topics and activities. Please realize that the activities are simply tools for meeting the overall goals of a support group: helping the students understand how chemical dependence has affected them, encouraging them to make healthy changes in their behaviors, and helping them to grow in self-esteem. In many sessions, alternative activities are listed. Feel free to use or not use them. After becoming familiar with support groups you might want to experiment with other activities as well. Note in particular that some of the sessions are built around a certain film. While a film can be a very effective teaching tool, you sometimes may not have access to the one suggested. Hence alternative activities are listed whenever a film is suggested.

Whenever you use a worksheet it's important to discuss the group members' contributions to it. This kind of repetition increases the impact of the points discussed. Also, students discover that they're not alone—that, for example, they aren't the only ones who struggle with low self-esteem, fear, or other painful feelings.

Sessions are more productive when students sit on chairs placed in a small circle. Avoid chairs that have the writing surface attached to the front, since this will hinder openness. The two group leaders should sit on opposite sides of the circle, because one's blind spot is the area immediately to one's right or left, so students who occupy that area tend to receive the least amount of attention. Having the two leaders sit across from each other makes it easier to give all students equal attention.

Each of the following group formats was designed to fit into one group session. Forty-five-minute sessions make things a little tight; hour-long sessions are ideal.

Whenever possible, the group leaders should participate in all activities, including filling out the worksheets. It gives students the sense that you take all of this seriously and that you're part of the group.

## Activities Common to All Three Groups

Group warm-ups and closing activities are **basically** the same for all three kinds of support groups. Here are the important features of these two activities.

### Warm-ups

In both the Concerned Persons Group and the Drug Information Group, students might at first be hesitant to share their thoughts and feelings. So each of their sessions should begin with a group warm-up, which consists of a brief question like "What's a feeling that you have a hard time showing to others?" Warm-ups like that bring the group together and shift the focus from the head to the heart, from thinking to feeling. In a typical Recovery Group, however, warm-ups are used only when necessary. For example, when a new student joins the group, a group warm-up will ease any awkwardness the members might be feeling.

In the second week's session select a student to be in charge of the warm-up activity for the following week. At that session he or she should pick someone else for the week after, and so on. This way, the students are encouraged to take some responsibility for the group. Instruct them to keep the warm-ups brief (five minutes), because time is short and there's important ground to cover. Addendum 8.2 gives a list of group warm-ups. The students can either choose a warm-up from that list or create their own.

### Closing Activities

When the group session hasn't been very intense, you might not need a closing activity. But when there has been a lot of intense sharing, it's good to finish the session with a short activity that will reduce the intensity in the room. (This holds true for all three types of support groups.) There might be times when students have been crying or really taking risks in revealing their thoughts and feelings. If so, you wouldn't want to have things end suddenly with the bell ringing and everyone quickly getting up and leaving.

Instead, reserve the last five minutes for some activity to bring about an appropriate closure. Here are a few examples:

- "Something I learned about myself today is . . ."
- Tell a joke.
- Ask everyone to get up and stretch.
- Hold hands and be silent for three minutes.
- Tell the group members something you appreciate about them.
- Ask a member of the group to summarize what happened during the session.

### Format for a Concerned Persons Group

The following outline of the format for this group will give you a quick bird's-eye view of it; the explanation will then flesh out the details.

Outline of Format

**Session 1.**     **Group Goals and Rules**
　　　　　　　Goals:　　　　establish group rapport
　　　　　　　　　　　　　explain group rules
　　　　　　　Activity:　　Interview Activity

**Sessions 2-5.**　**Family History**
　　　　　　　Goals:　　　　validate personal experiences
　　　　　　　　　　　　　establish group unity
　　　　　　　　　　　　　familiarize leaders with
　　　　　　　　　　　　　　members' family histories
　　　　　　　Activity:　　Lifemaps

**Session 6.** **Feelings**
    Goals:        develop awareness of personal feelings
                     develop communication skills
    Activities:   The Stamp Game
                     My Own Feelings

**Session 7.** **Defenses**
    Goal:        identify personal defenses
    Activities:   My Two Sides
                     Ten Feelings

**Session 8.** **Chemical Dependence as a Disease**
    Goal:        present chemical dependence concepts
    Activities:   film—*Lots of Kids Like Us*
                     film—*Different Like Me*
                     book—*Different Like Me*

**Session 9.** **Detachment**
    Goal:        develop disengaging skills
    Activity:    discussion

**Session 10.** **Personal Needs**
    Goals:        identify personal needs
                     identify alternative methods of getting needs met
    Activities:   discussion
                     My Own Needs

**Session 11.** **Future Plans**
    Goals:        increase awareness of community resources
                     identify future goals
    Activities:   discussion
                     From Now On

**Session 12.**  **Closure**
  Goals:    build self-esteem
         facilitate group closure
  Activity:  Warm Fuzzy Bags

Explanation of Format

The following pages will explain the things you need to know
and do in each session.

*Session 1: Goals and Rules*

Most students participating in a group have absolutely no idea
of what to expect. They won't know what appropriate group
behavior is and might initially think that the group will be
similar to their classes. The first part of this session should be
spent explaining what belonging to a group entails, why they're
there, and what the rules for the group will be. Pass out a copy
of the rules for everyone to sign (Addendum 4.2a) and a
schedule for the first month's sessions (Addendum 4.1).

Since nervousness and embarrassment will initially be the
predominant feelings, the first session is designed to help the
students begin to feel comfortable with each other. A good
icebreaker is an activity called the Interview Activity (Addendum 8.3). This is a list of questions for group members to ask
each other. Pair members of the group—preferably with someone they don't know very well—and instruct them to ask each
other the questions on the sheet you've handed out. After
everyone has finished (give them fifteen minutes to do this),
come back into a circle and ask each person to introduce his or
her partner to the rest of the group and share their recorded
responses.

## Sessions 2-5:  Family History

An excellent way to bring about group cohesion is to encourage members to discuss their families and their backgrounds. Hearing one group member talk about Dad coming home drunk or Mom ending up in treatment will give the rest of the group permission to talk about their "secrets." The Lifemaps activity will encourage this process.

Pass out blank sheets of newsprint paper and markers and allow the students an entire group session to draw the chronological history of their lives—from when they were born to the present. They should include anything significant to them: moving, parents' divorce, Dad coming home drunk and yelling at everyone, first kiss, changing schools, etc. Undoubtedly they'll want to know how to record this information, so discuss a few possible methods: **linear progression**—construct a timeline, placing significant events in chronological order; **boxed captions**—draw squares and sketch different scenes in each; **journal entries**—some students won't want to draw, so let them write out the events and their feelings. Encourage them to be creative, but make sure they understand the importance of including their own feelings associated with the past events.

The next three sessions should be used to discuss the Lifemaps. Give each member a reasonable amount of time to discuss his or her Lifemap with the group. Ask two other members of the group to hold the student's Lifemap for the rest of the group to see while he or she explains the contents. If they're hesitant to share, or if they skip over things, slow them down by asking questions. Typically, group members will want to give only superficial information: "This happened, and then that happened, and then my brother . . ." This isn't what you want them to do. Ask questions that encourage students to identify and express feelings: "How did you feel when your brother did that? What was the feeling when your mom left your dad?"

Encourage other group members to ask questions too; this will set the stage for the group to function as a team rather than having the leader always asking the questions.

You should cover between two and three Lifemaps in each session. Discussing more than three Lifemaps in one session means you're moving too quickly; instead, ask additional questions and encourage the students to talk in greater depth. Fewer than two means the students are sharing quite a bit, but it also means that you'll be processing Lifemaps for weeks to come. Don't devote more than three sessions to this activity.

## Session 6: Feelings

Identifying and understanding feelings is the foundation of this group. Many students with chemically dependent parents, having grown up in an environment where feelings aren't acknowledged or discussed, are aware of only a limited range of them, such as being happy or angry. It's crucial that you be able to help them get in touch with their own feelings by being aware of the wide range of feelings that all people can experience.

The following extended passage entitled "Our Mysterious Feelings" is taken from Chapter 5 of the book *Parenting for Prevention* by David Wilmes. (See Resources.)

### Our Mysterious Feelings

To start with, let it be clear that our feelings are bodily responses that originated in our ancestors' instinctive physical responses to the world around them— for instance, in the fight-or-flight instinct we all still experience when we sense danger stalking us. We've all noticed the physical responses characteristic of deep feelings, such as quick breaths, pounding heart, clenched fists. Our everyday language, too, recognizes the physical basis of feelings: When we mention our "gut reaction" to something, we're speaking quite precisely. Feelings are very much of the body. And there's the rub. These bodily, animal reactions of ours are very familiar and yet very mysterious and disturbing. Like the wild animals themselves, they're immensely powerful, unpredictable, hard to control. Over the centuries, then, we humans have often handled them in inappropriate ways. Sometimes we've given in totally to their urgings and indulged in orgies of drunkenness, sex, or wholesale slaughter. At other times, frightened by those excesses, we've tried to suppress our feelings entirely, pretending they don't even exist, or at best have been quite suspicious of them.

In recent decades our culture has been struggling to give feelings their proper role in a balanced life, but the old battle goes on; and frankly, most of today's kids know very little about feelings and how to handle them. That's precisely why we need to help them develop lifeskills in that crucial area: When kids are tempted to get into chemicals, they're almost invariably having problems with their feelings, not with their intellects.

### The Three Stages of Processing Our Feelings

To get down to basics in understanding feelings and helping our kids understand them and deal successfully with them, let's talk about the three stages we need to go through to reach some mastery in this area: identifying feelings, owning them, and expressing (sharing) them.

#### Identifying Feelings

As we've mentioned, it's often quite easy to know when others are experiencing feelings, especially deep ones. Flashing eyes, scowls, a red face can be sure

93

tipoffs. But when we're all stirred up inside, what are we really feeling? Recognizing and identifying our own feelings can be very difficult. Younger kids usually have to settle for something vague such as "I feel ishy" or "I feel bad." With help, though, even preschoolers can master simple ways of naming their feelings: "mad," "sad," "glad," for instance.

Once kids move into grade school they can usually begin to recognize and identify a wider range of feelings. As kids develop their capacity to recognize and identify feelings, it's important that we expose them to an increasingly larger vocabulary of feeling words. Here's a sample:

| | | | |
|---|---|---|---|
| afraid | elated | irritated | satisfied |
| aggressive | enraged | jealous | scared |
| alarmed | enthusiastic | joyful | secure |
| amused | envious | lonely | shocked |
| angry | exasperated | loved | smug |
| annoyed | excited | mad | surprised |
| anxious | frightened | miserable | tense |
| appreciated | frustrated | needed | terrified |
| bitter | furious | nervous | threatened |
| bored | glad | paranoid | thrilled |
| calm | guilty | perplexed | troubled |
| cautious | happy | powerful | uneasy |
| comfortable | helpless | powerless | unimportant |
| concerned | hopeful | puzzled | unloved |
| confident | hopeless | regretful | unneeded |
| confused | horrified | rejected | unsure |
| contented | hostile | relieved | wanted |
| crushed | hurt | resentful | worried |
| disappointed | inadequate | respected | worthless |
| discouraged | inspired | sad | worthwhile |
| eager | insecure | safe | |

*Owning Feelings*

By "owning" feelings we simply mean acknowledging them as **ours**, acknowledging that they spring from **us** and are a part of **us**. Whether someone insults us and we react by feeling angry or embarrassed, or whether someone praises us and we react by feeling elated, what results is **our** feeling.

That may sound obvious, but it isn't. What often happens is that we in effect act as if our feeling is ultimately the responsibility of the **other** person. Laura says to Jack, "You made me mad because you said I cheated on the math exam, and I didn't." While we can sympathize with such an outburst, we need to recognize that blaming our feeling on someone else, making it the other's "property," is a copout. Why? Well, suppose that Jack made the very same accusation against Jeanne, but Jeanne very calmly (though firmly) denied it, with no anger. Since she came up with a response different from Laura's, it couldn't be merely Jack's accusation that **made** Laura angry; what made the difference was **Laura's** reaction: the way **she** took it and responded to it.

What that means is that we, not others, are ultimately responsible for our feelings. It's a hard lesson to learn, but it's true, and as we help our kids to see and accept that truth, we're showing them how to take control of their own lives: **I'm** the one who decides how I feel and act; I'm not at the mercy of what others decide about how I'm going to feel and act. At the same time, of course, the comforting realization that **I'm** in control of my own life means that I'm accepting **responsibility** for my feelings. That's a big step toward maturity.

We can also help our kids see that their feelings are their friends. How? By showing them that their feelings send them signals about how they're relating at the moment to persons, places, things, or circumstances. Teach them to ask themselves questions such as, **How** do I feel these days about my appearance? If I feel lousy about it, why? Am I just imagining that I'm too fat or that my clothes aren't right? And what's **behind** my feelings? Maybe I do need to eat healthier, non-fattening foods; maybe I do need some sound advice on how to dress; maybe I do need to wear less makeup or buy clothes that work for **me**, not for someone else. How do I feel about my classes? If I'm feeling pretty happy, maybe my feelings are signaling me that I'm a conscientious kid who deserves to feel good about my studies.

*Expressing Feelings*

We can of course express our feelings in many ways: in artworks, poetry, stories, music, for instance. But it's absolutely indespensable that our kids develop skills in expressing their feelings in the way in which practically everyone expresses them every day: by the spoken word. Learning to say out loud "I feel hurt" or "I feel good" is a fundamental lifeskill, because without the ability to verbalize our feelings we'll find ouselves alone, cut off from the support and concern that only relationships with people can provide. And those relationships depend heavily on our ability to communicate our feelings in spoken words.

By learning to express feelings we're reaching out to others and building a bridge that creates the intimacy, togetherness, rapport, and mutual support we all need. Kids who can't **express** their feelings in that coin of the realm, speech, are clearly more vulnerable to using chemicals to **change** their feelings.

An easy tool to help kids and to help ourselves to model appropriate handling of feelings is "I statements" such as "I feel hurt," "I feel happy," "I feel afraid." These "I statements" are nothing more than statements that begin with "I," name a feeling, and give a brief explanation. For instance, "I felt let down when I found you hadn't finished raking the lawn before you went out with Rick." By modeling statements that show we can identify, own, and express our feelings, we're teaching our kids a basic lifeskill.

In Session 6 the goal is to help students identify and understand the many different types of emotions they've actually experienced.

Begin this session by asking the students to name as many feelings as they can, including an example of what the feeling word means. Follow with an activity that challenges the students to talk about different feelings they've experienced and in what situations they've experienced those feelings. Here are two activities that work very well.

**The Stamp Game:** In the Stamp Game, students select feelings cards representative of their emotional makeup (e.g., a student might have a large pile of anger cards, a few guilt cards, and one fear card) and then discuss their stack of cards with the group by explaining why, for example, they have so many anger cards and what the fear cards are for. Other variations on this theme are provided in the *Stamp Game* kit by Claudia Black. (See Resources, subhead Other.)

**My Own Feelings:** An alternative activity is My Own Feelings (see Addendum 8.4). First ask the students to fill out the worksheet. Then go around the circle and ask each group member to share with the rest of the support group what he or she has written.

## Session 7: Defenses

Growing up in a chemically dependent home requires a defensive posture in order to protect oneself from otherwise-painful feelings. Most of these students will have cut themselves off from their emotions and from what goes on in their family because it simply hurts too much. This is a normal reaction, given their present circumstances.

Unfortunately, these patterns are often used when they're not appropriate; they become a way of life. Perhaps the most typical reaction is simple withdrawal. Many children with chemically dependent parents simply turn off their feelings (at least on the outside). They don't show much reaction to anything around them, either positive feelings or negative ones. Or some kids appear angry most of the time. Instead of feeling sad, they scowl; instead of feeling scared, they yell. Still other kids become compulsive clowns. Eveything is funny. They tease other students, they laugh at inappropriate times, they can't sit still. And of course there's the common defense that fools quite a few adults—the "everything's perfect" defense. These students put large amounts of energy into creating the facade that absolutely nothing is wrong in their lives. And often it doesn't appear that there is:  perfect grades, busy all the time, never a sad face. The true story, however, is a frightened, guilt-ridden child who thinks "If only I do everything just right, work real hard and pretend, things are sure to get better at home." (See Addendum 8.11 for a further description of defenses that children with chemically dependent parents develop.)

An important first step in letting go of these defense roles is to help students identify what defenses they use. Then start a discussion with questions such as "When do you use this defense?" and "Does using this defense help you, or hurt you?"

Here are two activities that will help students identify defenses they use frequently:

**My Two Sides:** Ask the students to draw a large outline shape of themselves on newsprint. If the newsprint sheet is large enough, they can lie down on the paper and have a friend trace the outlines of their body on the paper. Inside the figure they should detail the feelings they keep to themselves; outside the figure, the feelings they reveal to the world around them. After everyone has done this, discuss the disparity between the inside and outside by asking questions like "What feelings do you have hidden inside? How do you present yourself to the world? How great is the difference between your insides and outsides?"

**Ten Feelings:** Addendum 8.5 is a worksheet that will help students identify why some feelings are easy for them to share and others are difficult. After they've had time to finish the worksheet, go around the circle and ask them to share what they've written. Time permitting, ask them to relate an instance that involved using a defense to cover up a feeling listed on their worksheet.

*Session 8: Chemical Dependence as a Disease*

Students often know very little about the disease concept of chemical dependence. They don't understand blackouts, why their parents don't just quit drinking or using other drugs, what treatment is for or what happens at an Alcoholics Anonymous meeting. An excellent way to convey these concepts is to show a film. *Lots of Kids Like Us* is a film designed for junior high school students. *Different Like Me* is another film appropriate for both junior and senior high school students. (See Resouces.)

After showing the film, reinforce concepts that were presented, such as trying to throw away the alcohol or the importance of taking care of yourself. Ask students questions about the characters in the film—e.g., "What did the children in the film do to take care of themselves? How did their parents' drinking affect them? What would you do if you were in their shoes?" The discussion guide that comes with *Different Like Me* will be very helpful.

As an alternative to showing a film, read a few sections, including the section on co-dependence, out of the book *Different Like Me: For Teens Who Worry About Their Parents' Use of Alcohol/Drugs*. (See Resources.)

*Session 9: Detachment*

When the chemically dependent people in group members' families are being particularly troublesome, the children need to know how to back off and separate themselves from the problem. They can't change their parents, but they can change how they react to the problem. This is called detaching, and it's an important skill for these students to learn. They need to understand that they needn't be upset just because Dad is in a rotten mood or Mom is drinking again. Their parents' problems don't have to be their problems.

The following description of detachment is found in the booklet *Detachment: The Art of Letting Go While Living With an Alcoholic*.

"The feelings of anger, shame, and guilt associated with family alcoholism or other drug dependence come from the constant confusion, conflict, unpredictability, inconsistency, mistrust, and sense of failure that each member experiences. The family victims seldom learn without outside help that they didn't cause the disease and that they can't control it.

"Literally, to save and enjoy their lives, **they need to do something positive**, something that will help them focus on their own problems and the help they need to get well. They need to shift the focus of their attention from the chemical and the chemically dependent parent to themselves: to their problems, their reactive behavior, and what they can do for themselves in their own recovery from this family disease. To free themselves for these positive steps in their return to a healthy life, these family members need to separate themselves from their reactive behavior and its causes. How? By developing the skill of **detachment."***

To help students develop that skill, discuss the concept of detaching and ask the students to identify previous personal experiences when their feelings and behaviors were affected by their parents' chemical dependence. Typical examples can include "The time when my dad came to pick me and my friends up from the movie and he was drunk" or "At night when I'm watching the television, my mom starts drinking and falls asleep next to me on the couch."

Ask the students to think of different ways they can detach themselves from the chemically dependent person's behavior. Typical scenarios will include a student deciding he doesn't need to argue with his dad when the dad is under the influence, or the student who realizes that giving her mom a kiss when she came home from school everyday to see if she could smell alcohol on her mom's breath only made her sad and angry when she discovered her mother had been drinking.

Another excellent book and film that give additional examples you can use in a support group is *Different Like Me*. (See Resources.)

---

*For more information on this subject read this entire booklet by Evelyn Leite. (See Resources.)

*Session 10: Personal Needs*

We all have needs. There are our physical needs, such as food, shelter, clothing, that keep us alive and warm. We also have emotional needs. Here is a small sample of common emotional needs:

- To be loved
- To feel appreciated
- To feel capable
- To be understood
- To be respected

- To feel safe
- To have time to be alone
- To have privacy
- To have time with friends
- To have fun

If these emotional needs aren't met, we get depressed, irritable, anxious, lonely. Kids are no different. But children in homes where there's chemical dependence not only don't get their emotional needs met; they don't even know they have such needs.

Session 10 is designed to help students identify their own emotional needs. First discuss what emotional needs are. Then ask the students to make a list of all the emotional needs people can have. Remind them that not everyone has exactly the same needs. After they finish this list, have them complete the My Own Needs worksheet (Addendum 8.6). After they've identified their own personal needs, ask them to rate how successful they are at getting their needs met. Use the remaining time to discuss the results.

*Session 11: Future Plans*

In one more week the support group will come to a close. But this isn't the end of the students' recovery progress—it's just the beginning. In review, we see that Sessions 2 through 8 created new awarenesses for the students, Session 9 showed them how to detach from the chemically dependent family member, and Session 10 helped them to identify personal needs. Session 11 will help them put into practice what they've learned.

102

The hallmark of many children with chemically dependent parents is passivity:  i.e., being harmfully affected by the chemical dependence in their families without offering any opposition or resistance to it, feeling confused and alone, not getting their own needs met. This session is designed to encourage them to think of ways to turn this passivity around. Here are a few common examples students will offer:

- I talk to my parents about how I'm feeling about the drinking.
- I get out of the house when the drinking starts.
- I go to Alateen or a church group.
- I talk with close friends about how I'm feeling.
- I practice detaching.
- I find friends who help me feel good about myself.
- I talk with the school guidance counselor.
- I do something fun to get my mind off the problem at home.

Ask the students to make a list of all the things they can do to help them take care of themselves. Suggest any important ideas they forget. When the list is finished, ask them to complete the From Now On worksheet, Addendum 8.7. When everyone is through, ask the students to share their worksheets with the rest of the group.

After meeting with these students eleven sessions in a row, you probably will have specific concerns about some of the members. For example, you might notice that Danny talks often about how the constant arguing at home bothers him, or that Betsy spends a lot of time worrying about how much her mother is drinking. If these students don't address these issues on their worksheets, bring them to their attention.

*Session 12: Closure*

The last session is the time to say goodbye and bring the group to a close. Warm Fuzzy Bags is an exercise that will allow group members to give each other compliments and say their good-byes. Hand out paper lunch bags for everyone to decorate with markers. While they're doing this, explain that warm fuzzies are **specific** compliments and other things we say to each other that make the other person feel good. Discuss examples of warm fuzzies such as "I really admire your honesty," "I appreciate the way you respect everyone's feelings," and "You're a very good listener." Then give the members enough slips of paper that they can write a warm fuzzy for each person in the group, putting the slip of paper into the student's bag when they're done. When the group is over, everyone will have lots of compliments and warm goodbyes from the rest of the group to take home.

An excellent source of additional group closure activities can be found on pages 305-311 of the Shelley MacKay Freeman prevention curriculum *From Peer Pressure to Peer Support*. (See Resources.)

This last session is an appropriate time for any post-group evaluations (these are discussed in Chapter 9 and Addendum 9).

### Format for a Drug Information Group

The following outline of the format for this group will give you a quick bird's-eye view of it; the explanation will then flesh out the details.

Outline of Format

**Session 1.**   **Group Goals and Rules**
Goals:          establish group rapport
                explain group rules
Activity:       Interview Activity

**Session 2.** **History of Students' Chemical Use**
          Goal:            identify history of chemical use
          Activities:     History of My Chemical Use
                             discussion

**Session 3.** **Reasons for Using Chemicals**
          Goal:            identify relationship between
                             feelings and chemical use
          Activities:     film—*Story About Feelings*
                             film—*Where's Shelley?*
                             discussion
                             Chemicals and Feelings

**Session 4.** **Defenses**
          Goal:            identify defenses related to
                             chemical use
          Activity:       Chemicals and Defenses

**Session 5.** **Consequences**
          Goal:            identify consequences related
                             to chemical use
          Activity:       discussion

**Session 6.** **Chemical Dependence in the Family**
          Goals:           identify students affected by
                             family chemical dependence
                             understand effects of chemical
                             dependence on the family
          Activities:     film—*My Father's Son*
                             questionnaire
                             Survival Roles

**Session 7.** **Closure**
          Goals:           final personal assessment
                             develop plans and goals

| Activities: | feedback from peers and group leaders |
| | referrals to other groups or outside agencies |

## Explanation of Format

The following pages will explain the things you need to know and do in each session.

### Session 1: Introduction

The initial meeting of this type of group is overcast with some anxiety and nervous energy. After handing out and explaining a copy of the rules (Addendum 4.2b) and a group schedule (Addendum 4.1), spend the remainder of the session discussing why the students are in this group. This will give you a sense of the mood of the students and their problems. It will also help reduce tension in the room. Go around the circle, asking the students to explain why they're there and how they feel about being in the group. Encourage them to be open and express any negative feelings they might have. Let them know you won't take it personally; after all, it isn't your fault that they must be in this support group! If they offer only a few cursory comments, ask them for more detail with questions like "How do your parents feel about your being here?" and "Do you think you need to be here?"

### Session 2: History of Students' Chemical Use

As the group leader, you want to be aware of group members' experiences with mind-altering chemicals; you also want them to be aware of this information—spread out in front of them on a time continuum from the first time they used to the present. All too often, students abusing chemicals repress most of their previous using episodes, instead remembering only bits and pieces.

Ask them to complete the History of My Chemical Use worksheet (Addendum 8.8), answering any questions they might have about how to fill it out correctly. After they've finished, spend the remaining time going around the circle asking the students to share their worksheets with the rest of the group. All worksheets and tests given during a group session should be collected at the end of the session. Make it clear to them that you won't show the worksheets to anyone and that they'll be getting all their paperwork back during the last session.

*Session 3: Reasons for Using Chemicals*

It's important that the students make a connection between their feelings and their behavior associated with chemical use. With this insight can come the awareness that there are more effective and constructive ways to change or resolve feelings than through using a mind-altering chemical. The goal of this session is that students will understand that people use chemicals to change how they feel and that they'll be able to identify what feelings they want to change when they use chemicals. (Feelings are discussed in more detail in Session 6 of the Concerned Persons Group format.)

Begin Session 3 with a film, either *A Story About Feelings* or *Where's Shelley?* Both films are available through Johnson Institute and are listed in Resources. Although these films are geared to younger children, they both effectively establish the connection between chemicals and feelings. After showing the film, ask the students to make on the chalkboard a list of feelings (e.g., feeling bored, lonely, shy, angry) that people use chemicals to change. Ask group members to pick out which feelings they most often change through the use of chemicals. If group members are honest, many will identify feelings such

107

as anger, fear, sadness, loneliness, and the fear of not fitting in. It's these types of feelings that make students feel uncomfortable and that they therefore want to change by drinking or using other drugs.

If it isn't possible to show either film, a different but equally effective activity would be to instruct students to complete and then discuss the Chemicals and Feelings worksheet of Addendum 8.9.*

*Session 4: Defenses*

When students start abusing mind-altering chemicals, negative consequences follow. At first the consequences might take only the form of uncomfortable feelings: guilt, paranoia, general uneasiness. If they continue to abuse chemicals, other more noticeable consequences come into play. Relationships with nonusing friends are strained or cut off, parents become suspicious about changes in behavior, school performance starts to fall. Students abusing chemicals will continue using even though the chemicals are causing them problems. In order to keep things under control they develop a defensive posture that provides a buffer between them and increasingly painful reality. The worse things become, the more they turn to the chemicals for relief. Defenses are what distort reality for the students so that this abusive cycle can continue.

Students participating in a Drug Information Group are apt to have developed many defenses already. Asking them to take a look at the defenses they use is important because when the defenses are uncovered they can make an honest appraisal of their chemical use and its effects on their life.

Ask the support group members to read and complete the

---

* This worksheet is from the workbook *Can I Handle Alcohol/Drugs?* by David Zarek and James Sipe. This self-assessment guide contains other appropriate activities for any Drug Information Group. (See Resources.)

Chemicals and Defenses worksheet (Addendum 8.10). Afterward, ask them to share their answers with the rest of the support group. Don't be afraid to be confrontative during this session if some of the group members are hesitant to identify defenses they use. If a student says he or she doesn't use any defenses, then ask another student to share his or her sheet first. When this person is finished, return to the resisting student and ask if he or she could relate to any of the examples the other person had shared. Typically this person will be able to relate to at least one of them.

*Session 5: Consequences*

All students in a Drug Information Group have experienced consequences from their chemical use or they wouldn't be attending this group: consequences ranging from poor grades to wrecked friendships, from loss of interest in activities to strained family relations.

After introducing this topic of consequences, ask the students to compile on the chalkboard a list of possible consequences. Spend the remaining time going around the circle asking students to identify consequences they've experienced as a result of their chemical use. Many times students hesitate to admit consequences other than legal ones. If they do, you'll need to be direct, asking questions like "How has your family been affected by your chemical use? How are your grades now compared to what they were before you started using chemicals? What happened to your old group of friends after you got involved in smoking pot?" Don't be afraid to be confrontative. If you really want to be effective, do a little homework before the group session. Get a printout of the students' grade history for the past few years and other data that you can use to enlighten them if their memories aren't working properly.

There will usually be at least a few students in a Drug Information Group who have chemically dependent parents, because children raised in such a family run a high risk of developing chemical dependence. And no wonder. Many of them have seen parents turn to alcohol or other drugs when they needed to change their feelings. These early childhood memories are coupled with the feelings of low self-worth, frustration, shame, and sadness that children with a chemically dependent parent have usually experienced. Simply put, these are young persons whose primary role models turned to chemicals for support. Such students are a new generation of chemical dependents in the making.

The primary goal of Session 6 is to reach out to these high-risk students. Any students in a Drug Information Group whom you discover to have chemically dependent parents should be referred to the support-group coordinator or school counselor so that other actions can be taken, such as placement in a Concerned Persons group or in individual counseling. The secondary goal of this session is to provide some basic education about chemical dependence and family dynamics for those students in the group who haven't had any experience with this problem.

*My Father's Son* is a film that clearly demonstrates the connection between a parent's chemical dependence and a son's drinking problem. (See Resources.) After showing it, discuss whether the group members think the adolescent who appears at the end of the movie will develop a drinking or other drug problem like his father. Why or why not? Finish the session by handing out the questionnaire of Addendum 7. Any student who has more than three "yes" answers should be talked to individually because there's a good chance that there's a drinking or other drug problem in this student's family.

If it isn't possible to show the film, hand out the Survival

Roles worksheet of Addendum 8.11 for the students to read. The last page has a worksheet for them to complete. Discuss the roles after they've finished the worksheet.

*Session 7: Closure*

The last session of the group is a review of the previous sessions. It's an opportunity for all students to discuss concerns about their chemical use and what they intend to do about it. First, hand back the collection of worksheets for each student. Then after they've looked at all the worksheets they've completed and have reviewed what they've learned, ask them to tell the rest of the group whether they think their chemical use is a problem for them. Ask them to explain their answers. Challenge the students to defend their self-assessment (even if you agree with it).

Then ask the other group members to give the student feedback. Do they agree? Why or why not? Keep asking questions; don't let them get away with simple, incomplete responses.

This can be a powerful session, especially when the group is courageous enough to let a particular person know that they all believe he or she has a problem. You should add your own opinions to the discussion, basing them on what you observed during the course of the group.

Finish the session by asking each student if he or she plans to make any changes in chemical use, and if so, what the changes will be. Any post-group evaluations (discussed in Chapter 9 and Addendum 9) should be given at the end of this session.

## Format for a Recovery Group

No outline of this group's format is needed, because most Recovery Groups are relatively unstructured.

Start each session by having everyone "check in." Ask students to share how their week went, whether they've been staying sober, and if they need any time to talk in the group. Encouraging students to tell the group they need time is important for two reasons: It helps students practice taking responsibility for their own needs, and it ensures that students who need time to talk will get it.

Often, students "checking in" and telling the group they need some time precludes the need for a discussion topic. Most students usually will have something on their minds. When this isn't the case, the group leader can introduce topics such as parental chemical dependence, relationships, dangers of relapse, grieving over losses, regular attendance at meetings, personal inventories, and peer support. Here are some discussion topics to get you started:

• **Why Did I Quit Using Chemicals?**   It's helpful for students to understand the reasons why they quit using. It's also beneficial for the rest of the group to hear about the struggles their peers have had with chemicals.

• **What Is My Program of Recovery?**   Sometimes, recovering students aren't aware of what they should and shouldn't do in order to stay sober. Encourage them to construct a personal program in order to ensure that they maintain sobriety. Challenge them to verbalize what their personal recovery programs entail. One student might report that all she does is go to a weekly N.A. meeting; another might say that he attends A.A., works the twelve steps, goes to aftercare, and gets support from his friends and girlfriend. Everyone will have his or her own personal plan.

• **Symptoms of a Relapse.** Ask students  to make a list of symptoms that would indicate when a person was building up to a relapse and would start using chemicals once again. What should they do if they're close to relapsing or if they do relapse? What should they do if a friend relapses?

• **My Family.** Typically, a chemically dependent adolescent's family has gone through quite a bit of turmoil. This turmoil may or may not have been resolved. Asking students to talk about how their family members get along with and communicate with one another—e.g., both before they quit using and after—is sure to get a discussion started.

• **Relationships.** Ask the students to discuss the pros and cons of relationships, including different types. One student might talk about the problems of interacting with friends who use chemicals. Another might bring up the importance of making sure you "work your program" and go to a regular meeting, even though you're madly in love with someone. Another might point out that he was told it's best to avoid intimate relationships until he had been in recovery for awhile. Ask the other students if they agree.

• **My Boundaries.** Pass out rolls of masking tape and instruct the support group members to mark off borders on the floor indicating what they need for personal space. Some might mark off a small circle; others might want half of the room. Ask questions about what you observe: "Why do you have so much space and she has so little? What does that say about you? Is that good or bad?"

A valuable workbook to use in a Recovery Group is *Breaking Away: Saying Goodbye to Alcohol/Drugs* by Jean Sassatelli, R.N. (See Resources.)

*Addendum 8.1*

# Session Outline

Type of Support Group:

**Outline of Session number____**

Session title:

Goal(s) of this session:

Group Activities:

Materials needed:

Warm-up and closing activities:

Things to do after the session:

Notes:

*Addendum 8.2*

# Warm-ups

Name one feeling that's easy for you to talk about and one that's difficult.

Are you more like your mother, or your father?  Why?

Communicate nonverbally how you're feeling today.

When somebody hurts your feelings, what do you do?

What do you do when you're angry?

Tell the group one thing you appreciate about yourself.

After everyone is sitting in a tight circle, have them turn to the right and gently massage the neck of the person next to them.

> **Note:** You might be surprised how uncomfortable some students are with touching or being touched. This warm-up won't work in every group, nor should it be used in a group's initial stage.

If you were an animal, which kind would you be? Why?

Demonstrate your personality when you were a little child.

Name one physical quality of yours that you like.

Identify one quality of yours that can be helpful to a friend.

When was the last time you cried? What were the tears about?

When you really need to talk to somebody, whom do you turn to?

What's one thing that people don't understand about you?

When you need time to be alone, where do you go, and what do you do?

*Addendum 8.3*

# Interview Activity

Ask your partner these questions, and write the answers next to the questions on your sheet.

1. What's your name?

2. Where were you born?

3. What do you like to do in your spare time?

4. What's something that really bugs you?

5. If you had five thousand dollars, what would you do with it?

6. What's your favorite music group?

7. What one word would best describe you?

8. What are you looking forward to this year?

9. What aren't you looking forward to this year?

10. What are you afraid of?

Now think of two additional questions to ask your partner:

11. Question:

    Answer:


12. Question:

    Answer:

# My Own Feelings

Five feelings are listed below. Lots of times kids living in a home where there's an alcohol or other drug problem have experienced these different feelings and many others. For each feeling listed, mention a time you've had that feeling. At the bottom of the sheet are two blanks for you to fill in by naming two other feelings you've experienced. Then, as with the others, mention a time you've had those feelings.

A time I felt **angry** was:

A time I felt **happy** was:

A time I felt **scared** was:

A time I felt **sad** was:

A time I felt **guilty** was:

A time I felt _____ was:

A time I felt _____ was:

# Ten Feelings

In the blanks provided, write in ten feelings. Then next to each feeling word you wrote, tell why the feeling is easy or difficult to reveal to other people.

Five feelings easy for me to reveal to others are:

1. _____

2. _____

3. _____

4. _____

5. _____

Five feelings difficult for me to reveal to others are:

1. _____

2. _____

3. _____

4. _____

5. _____

# My Own Needs

Everyone has emotional needs. What are yours? They might be different from everyone else's. Think about this for a moment and then in the left-hand column write down six of your needs. Then complete the right-hand side of the worksheet. Next to each of the emotional needs you identified, rate how often this need is met.

My emotional needs are:

|  | Never | Sometimes | Always |
|---|---|---|---|
| 1. _____ | 1  2  3 | 4  5  6  7 | 8  9  10 |
| 2. _____ | 1  2  3 | 4  5  6  7 | 8  9  10 |
| 3. _____ | 1  2  3 | 4  5  6  7 | 8  9  10 |
| 4. _____ | 1  2  3 | 4  5  6  7 | 8  9  10 |
| 5. _____ | 1  2  3 | 4  5  6  7 | 8  9  10 |
| 6. _____ | 1  2  3 | 4  5  6  7 | 8  9  10 |

*Addendum 8.7*

# From Now On . . .

On this worksheet list the things you'll do differently in view of what you've learned in this support group.

1. From now on,                    instead
   I'm going to _____        of _____

2. From now on,                    instead
   I'm going to _____        of _____

3. From now on,                    instead
   I'm going to _____        of _____

4. From now on,                    instead
   I'm going to _____        of _____

5. From now on,                    instead
   I'm going to _____        of _____

# History of My Chemical Use

The worksheet on the next page is a summary of your experiences with mind-altering chemicals—how much and how often, both past and present. Under the Past category, fill in how old you were when you first used that chemical and then how much and how often you used it during the first year. Under the Present category, fill in how much and how often you currently use that chemical. Do this for every chemical you've used.

Name _____ Date _____

| Chemical | Past | | | Present | |
| (The first line is filled in as an example.) | Age | Amount | Frequency | Amount | Frequency |
| Alcohol | 13 | 3 beers | once a wk. | 6 beers | twice a wk. |
| Alcohol (beer, wine, liquor) | | | | | |
| Marijuana (pot, hash, hash oil) | | | | | |
| Uppers (speed, crystal, crosstops) | | | | | |
| Downers (ludes, barbs, tranquilizers) | | | | | |
| Hallucinogens (LSD, acid, mushrooms) | | | | | |
| Inhalants (glue, gasoline, rush) | | | | | |
| Codeine (in cough syrup or in pain medication) | | | | | |
| Heroin (smack) | | | | | |
| Cocaine (snow, crack) | | | | | |
| PCP (angel dust) | | | | | |
| Other (specify: _____ | | | | | |

# Chemicals and Feelings

Our feelings are our emotional responses to what we're thinking or doing or to what's happening to us. Our moods are made up of many feelings. Some of our feelings—such as sadness, shame, and anger—are painful, so we usually try to avoid them. Other feelings—such as love, excitement, pride, and happiness—are pleasurable, so we naturally like to experience them. Most people experience a wide range of feelings and moods in a typical day.

Many people learn that chemicals (alcohol, marijuana, "uppers," or whatever) can give them good feelings and moods. They also learn that they usually return to feeling "normal" after the effects of chemicals wear off.

Unfortunately, many who've been regularly using chemicals find they can no longer cope with everyday feelings and situations without the chemicals. This is because they've learned to rely on chemicals to help them express certain feelings (for example, they feel confident or courageous after using alcohol) or to help them cover unwanted feelings (they feel less stress or anxiety after using marijuana). When people begin to rely on chemicals, they often find it hard to admit or express their true feelings **even when they're not using them.**

Below is a list of some basic feelings. Tell about a time when you've felt this way.

Angry:

Sad:

Happy:

Scared:

Ashamed:

Guilty:

Check the proper column to indicate how often you usually experience each of these feelings.

|         | Never | Seldom | Rather Often | Very Often |
|---------|-------|--------|--------------|------------|
| **Angry**   |       |        |              |            |
| **Sad**     |       |        |              |            |
| **Happy**   |       |        |              |            |
| **Scared**  |       |        |              |            |
| **Ashamed** |       |        |              |            |
| **Guilty**  |       |        |              |            |

*Addendum 8.10*

# Chemicals and Defenses[*]

People naturally develop defenses to protect themselves from threatening or uncomfortable thoughts, feelings, or situations. This is a normal process that helps them cope with fear, frustration, anxiety, and conflict.

We use defenses to **deny** or "change" reality to prevent ourselves from becoming aware of painful thoughts, to avoid painful feelings, to escape situations that are threatening (or seem to be), and to protect ourselves from facing the unpleasant consequences of our own behavior.

For example, Dawne occasionally babysat her younger brother after school. One day Dawne's boyfriend James came over to take her for a ride in his new car. Although Dawne knew she shouldn't leave her brother at home alone, even for a moment, she rationalized going by telling herself, "I'll only be gone a little while. And anyway, my brother's taking a nap and won't even know I'm gone." Unfortunately for Dawne, while she was away her mother came home unexpectedly and was very frightened and angry to find her young son unattended.

When Dawne returned, her mother was furious and confronted Dawne about her irresponsible behavior. Then Dawne realized what she'd done. She felt guilty, admitted her mistake, and promised it would never happen again.

Dawne first used a defense, **rationalization**, to convince herself that it was OK to take a ride with her boyfriend. But when her mother confronted her with the reality of the situation, Dawne chose to accept reality (and to experience her feelings) rather than to continue rationalizing her wrongdoing.

---

[*]This activity is taken from the workbook *Can I Handle Alcohol/Drugs? A Self-Assessment Guide for Youth* by David Zarek and James Sipe. (See Resources.)

This is an example of a **normal defense**—a defense that the normal person wisely abandons when confronted with the real situation.

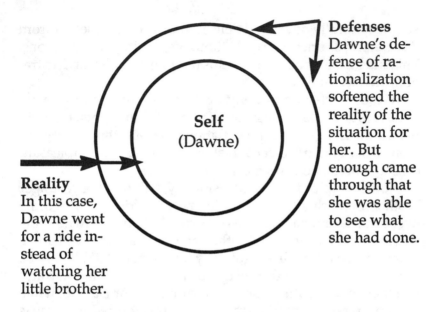

**Defenses**
Dawne's defense of rationalization softened the reality of the situation for her. But enough came through that she was able to see what she had done.

**Reality**
In this case, Dawne went for a ride instead of watching her little brother.

Self
(Dawne)

Normal defenses change the way we see a situation in order to make it "softer" or easier to deal with. However, one is still able to let in enough outside information about the real situation to adjust one's thinking, as Dawne did when her mother confronted her.

Steady chemical users, though, often become less able to accept painful reality, especially when confronted with the harmful consequences of their chemical use. This is partly because of the powerful "masking effects" of chemicals on feelings (see section 1) that cause a person to lose touch with the real situation. It also happens because as time goes on, steady chemical users' defenses become stronger and more rigid and therefore block out the insight they need if they're to change.

For example, Kevin was driving home from a party when he was stopped by the police because of his loud muffler. The officer smelled alcohol and give him a breath test that he failed. He was arrested and jailed overnight, was later found guilty, had to pay a fine, and had his license taken away.

Kevin felt no remorse and accepted no responsibility for his actions. He **minimized** the seriousness of the offense, **denied** having had more than three beers that night, and **blamed** his conviction on the "stupid cops who've got nothing better to do than hassle people who are just out for a good time." This is an example of using **rigid or harmful defenses.**

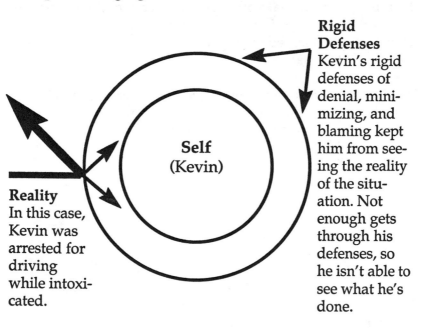

**Rigid Defenses**
Kevin's rigid defenses of denial, minimizing, and blaming kept him from seeing the reality of the situation. Not enough gets through his defenses, so he isn't able to see what he's done.

**Self (Kevin)**

**Reality**
In this case, Kevin was arrested for driving while intoxicated.

In this case, harmful defenses protected Kevin so completely that he filtered out all the painful information. As a result, he was really blind to his situation, so he wasn't able to change his behavior or to make amends.

Below are some common defenses used by steady chemical users. Answer the questions that follow.

**Denying:** refusing to recognize or accept reality.
How have you used denial to protect yourself from the consequences of your chemical use?

**Rationalizing:** inventing excuses so as to make unacceptable behavior seem acceptable.
How have you used rationalization to justify your chemical use?

**Blaming:** trying to make other people, places, or things responsible for the wrong things you've done.
How have you blamed other people, places, or things for your irresponsible behavior?

**Minimizing:** making something look less serious than it is.
How have you minimized what you've done or what's happened to you because of your chemical use?

*Addendum 8.11*

# Survival Roles of Children from Families Affected by Chemical Dependence

Family members of a chemically dependent person are also affected by his or her alcohol/other drug abuse. Living with someone who's chemically dependent can create many painful and confusing feelings such as anger, resentment, shame, guilt, hurt, loneliness, fear, and uncertainty about what will happen next.

As a result of such feelings, the children of chemically dependent persons tend to take on co-dependent behaviors or roles in order to shield themselves from their hurt. The inconsistent and unpredictable behavior of the alcohol/other drug-dependent person forces children to act and react in ways that help them to survive and that make life less painful.

Several of these co-dependent behaviors or roles are listed on the next two pages. Study them carefully and then answer the questions that follow.

|  | Outside Behavior (What you see; the visible traits) | Feelings (What you don't see; the inside story) | Payoff (What the child represents to the family; why members play along) |
|---|---|---|---|
| **The Family Hero/Heroine or Super Kid** | The little mother; the little man of the family; **always** does what's right; overachiever; overresponsible; needs everyone's approval; very serious; not much fun. | Feels hurt, inadequate; full of confusion, guilt, fear, low self-esteem; never feels he or she can do enough. | Provides self-worth to the family—someone to be proud of. |
| **The Problem Child or Scapegoat** | Hostile; tough; defiant; troublemaker; sullen; gets negative attention; sometimes uses chemicals. | Feels hurt and abandoned; feels anger and rejection; feels totally inadequate; no or low self-esteem. | Takes the focus off the real problem—see what he or she has done! |

| | | | |
|---|---|---|---|
| **The With-drawn Child or The Quiet One** | Loner; day dreamer; apathetic; withdrawn; drifts and floats through life; not missed for days; quiet, shy, ignored. | Feels unim-portant; not allowed to have feelings; lonely; feels hurt and abandoned; defeated; fearful. | Provides relief—strengthens illusion that "everything is all right in this family." |
| **The Family Clown or Family Mascot** | Super-cute, immature; anything for a laugh or attention; fragile and needful of protection; hyperactive; short atten-tion span; learning disabilities. | Low self-esteem; terrified; feels lonely, anx-ious, inade-quate, unim-portant. | Provides comic relief, fun, and humor; takes heat off the chemically dependent person. |

**Note:** Knowing these roles is useful because it can help us realize how chemical dependence in one family member can affect the other family members. The roles are not meant to be labels, and family members can adopt different survival roles at different times.

Some of the descriptions of the behavioral roles are taken from *The Family Trap* by Sharon Wegscheider (Rapid City: Nurturing Networks, 1988).

Answer and discuss the following questions:

1. If you come from a family affected by chemical dependence, can you identify with any one of the survivor roles?
   If so, which one? Explain.

2. Describe how you've acted out this role. Describe your
   real hidden feelings.

3. List the other children in your family and try to identify
   the roles each one acts out.

               Member                    Role

4. If you don't feel your family has a chemically dependent
   member, think of another family you know that may have
   a chemically dependent member (for example, relatives,
   friends, neighbors). List the children in that family and try
   to identify the role each one acts out.

               Member                    Role

*Chapter 9*

# What Happens After the Group Disbands?

Even though the hugs have been given and the goodbyes said during the final week of a group, the leader's work isn't over. Evaluations and recommendations need to be made for each member of your group. For some members, this might be the end of involvement with the group; for others, it will be just the beginning, because some form of additional help will be warranted. The group structure itself should also be examined and evaluated. How successful was the group experience? What could be done differently next time to make the group more effective?

Both these topics will be discussed in this chapter.

## Evaluating Individual Group Members

During the final session, inform the students that you'll be contacting them individually at a later time to discuss their individual needs. Before you meet with them individually, discuss possible ideas and concerns with your co-leader so you'll know beforehand what you'll be recommending.

Some members of your group will have learned what they needed to learn from the group, so no additional involvement is warranted. Make certain these students know that if they do have problems later, they'll be welcomed back into a support group. Other members will benefit from continued help in order to maintain their support system at the present level. These students should continue in a different group or in individual sessions with a school counselor. Unfortunately, there usually will be one or two in your group who need more intensive help than you or the school's support-group program can offer. These students should be referred for individual therapy, for chemical dependence evaluation, or for chemical dependence treatment.

It's usually not beneficial to place a student who finishes one group back into the same type of group, because the formats are identical and much of the experience would be redundant. However, switching to a different type of group can be beneficial.

If the student was initially referred to the group by someone—be it a school guidance counselor, parent, or community agency—you should contact this referral source before deciding on a recommendation. This contact could range from simply notifying the referral source that the student has completed group sessions, to inviting him or her to attend the follow-up meeting with the student. Which action should be taken must be determined on a case-by-case basis. If parents requested that their son be included in the Concerned Persons Group, for example, you should contact them so they know he has finished the support group. On the other hand, a referral to a Drug Information Group from the administration for a policy violation always warrants a post-group meeting with those involved to determine what, if any, further action should be taken.

Any actions that involve people or agencies outside the school should be done in concert with the school's counseling department. Whether it be a meeting with parents to express your concerns that their daughter receive therapy, or a referral to a chemical dependence treatment center, the guidance counselors are your connection to the community. Be clear on your boundaries.

## Concerned Persons Group: Recommendations

Concerned Persons Group members typically fall into one of two categories regarding future services. Many students who were once in the dark about their parents' chemical dependence now understand the problem and what they can and can't do about it. Many of these students won't need anything more. Typical examples of those who fit into this category are a student who hasn't seen his chemically dependent mother since he was two years old, and the student whose parent has been in recovery for many years. Unless these students demonstrate a need for future ongoing involvement in a support group, it's time to say goodbye and wish them well. You may also remind them that participating in Alateen or Al-Anon's ongoing twelve step program for family members can help them continue to remain healthy and grow.

Some of the students in a Concerned Persons Group are living in homes where they're confronted every day with the frustrating effects of chemical dependence. Many will need continued support and involvement in a support group. Time and resources allowing, it's beneficial—and rather a simple matter—to pool these students into a separate Concerned Persons Group (call it Concerned Persons Group II) that, instead of following a specific weekly format, allows them to discuss personal issues and maintain the support system they need to stay healthy. If providing a group such as this isn't possible, discuss other options such as their getting involved with a school guidance counselor, Alateen, Al-Anon, or other community support systems that could provide regular contact. (Community resources were discussed in Chapter 6.)

Occasionally there will be a student in your group who isn't able to keep his or her head above water. It might be a student who's extremely withdrawn and depressed, or one who you suspect, but can't prove, is being abused at home. These students should be referred to a therapist. If the student is amenable to the idea, set up a meeting between you, the student, and the school guidance counselor to explain your concerns and suggestions.


### Drug Information Group: Recommendations

Most students participating in a Drug Information Group were referred to the group by parents, teachers, or other caregivers. When the group disbands, a separate meeting should be scheduled for each group member.

These meetings will involve you, a school guidance counselor, the student's parents, and often a school administrator as well. The agenda for this meeting is to determine what should be done now that the student has completed group sessions. Possible alternatives for the student include being put on a no-use contract, being evaluated by an addiction counselor, being admitted to a chemical dependence treatment program, or being placed in a different kind of group such as a Concerned Persons Group or a Recovery Group.

If a student didn't attend every group session every week or was found under the influence while on a no-use contract, he or she probably should be referred for a chemical dependence evaluation. If the student did well in the group, is remaining abstinent, and wants to join a Recovery Group, that should be recommended.

Again, each case is different; but whatever decision is made, it's to be made in concert with other involved adults. Your contribution as a group leader is to report whether the student participated in the group, his or her attendance record for the seven sessions, and your impressions of the severity of his or her chemical use.*

## Recovery Group: Recommendations

Since a Recovery Group continues throughout the school year, the only official end to the group is at the year's close. It's assumed that those who aren't graduating will continue with the group in the fall. When students discontinue this group it's usually a sign that they've relapsed or are close to doing so. In this case, they must be confronted as soon as possible. If the reasons for their absence can't be remedied, their counselor(s) and parents should be notified.

## Evaluating the Group

Two primary variables that affect the success of a support group are the individual students and the group experience. You will have little control over the first variable. Some group members will undergo marked changes in behavior; others will change only slightly. Some students in a Drug Information Group will quit using chemicals as a result of their experiences in the group; a few will continue to use them, disregarding everything they've heard in the group. Some students will take risks in sharing thoughts, attitudes, and feelings and will gain

---

* For more information about contracting and intervention with young people, read *Choices and Consequences: What to Do When a Teenager Uses Alcohol/Drugs* by Dick Schaefer. (See Resources.)

personal insight; others will remain defensive and closed. You might witness a shy, hurting boy in a Concerned Persons Group start talking about feelings for the first time in his life, but you'll also experience the frustration of dealing with a student who, despite her plainly evident emotional pain, refuses to share anything remotely related to what she's feeling inside.

Fortunately, you **can** exert great control over the second variable, the group experience. As the group leader, you decide what's presented and how it's presented to the group. Furthermore, you can improve your presentation and leadership skills, modify the group activities, or change the discussion questions.

But when you want to find out how well the group format is doing, how do you do it?

One sure method of determining the efficacy of the group format is to ask students about their experience in the group. Was it helpful? Did they understand the presentations? Did they value the group's co-leaders? Any feedback students provide is valuable. Addendum 9 consists of a questionnaire soliciting group feedback.

Discuss this feedback and your own impressions of the group's success with your co-leader and in the support-group leaders' meetings. If, for example, a number of students report that a film was unrealistic and boring, you might want to experiment with a different film next time. Or if you and your co-leader thought the students in the previous Concerned Persons Group didn't quite understand why chemical dependence is called a disease, you may well decide to spend more time discussing the concept in future groups.

# Support-Group Feedback

To all group members:
Please take a minute to fill out this evaluation of your support group. Don't put your name on this sheet. Thank you.

I am a member of Support Group ___ (supply the letter).

Circle the numbers that apply. One is the lowest rating; ten is the highest.

1. Was your support group a valuable experience for you?

|  No | | | |  Maybe | | | |  Yes | |
|---|---|---|---|---|---|---|---|---|---|
| 1 | 2 | 3 | 4 | 5 | 6 | 7 | 8 | 9 | 10 |

2. How would you rate your support-group leaders' ability to lead the group?

| Poor | | | | | | | Excellent | | |
|---|---|---|---|---|---|---|---|---|---|
| 1 | 2 | 3 | 4 | 5 | 6 | 7 | 8 | 9 | 10 |

3. How helpful was your support-group leader for you?

| Of little help | | | | | Very helpful | | | | |
|---|---|---|---|---|---|---|---|---|---|
| 1 | 2 | 3 | 4 | 5 | 6 | 7 | 8 | 9 | 10 |

4. List three things you learned in your support group.

     a.

     b.

     c.

5. How did this support group help you?

6. How could this support group be improved?

# Afterword

Though the process of designing and conducting support groups might at first glance look difficult, once you get started the momentum will carry you along. At first there may be only one group of hesitant students and two nervous co-leaders, but these students will teach you about group process, and the next support group will be better.

As the support groups become accepted and established, the number of referrals will increase. Additional educators will be trained, and the number of groups will grow. As this happens, the faculty and the students will become more sensitive to the effects of chemical dependence, and the groups will reach students who would normally slip by unnoticed.

Maybe the groups won't be available to every student who needs them. Maybe some unexpected things will happen. Bringing chemical dependence services to school systems is in its early stages, so you're a pioneer. Even if you don't do everything right, or as well as you'd like, it will be worthwhile. Just giving students a chance to talk about their feelings and showing them alternatives is already a great step forward.

Many students need someone to ask them about their home life or to notice how everything has fallen apart for them now that they're smoking pot everyday. They need you to assure them that good things are just around the corner for them. They'll take part in the groups you've put into place and will start to talk about feelings and secrets they've never shared before. Belonging to a support group will expose them to new ideas and challenge them to try out new behaviors. For many of them, the groups will start profound and lifelong changes. You'll be inspired when you see new smiles and watch students resolve difficult situations. It really will work—and all of this from a few motivated educators, a circle of chairs, and some willing students. It's time to start.

# Resources

**Note:** Most of the following books, workbooks, booklets, films, and videocassettes on chemical dependence are quite recent and are available from the Johnson Institute. Since the Institute's address and phone numbers are given later in this section, we have not repeated that formal bibliographical data in every item listed below.

## Books

Anderson, Gary L. *When Chemicals Come to School: The Student Assistance Program Model.*

Cermak, Timmen L., M.D. *Diagnosing and Treating Co-dependence: A Guide for Professionals Who Work with Chemical Dependents, Their Spouses, and Children.*

Freeman, Shelley MacKay. *From Peer Pressure to Peer Support: Alcohol/Drug Prevention Through Group Process—A Curriculum for Grades 7-12.*

Johnson, Vernon E., D.D. *Intervention: How to Help Someone Who Doesn't Want Help—A Step-by-Step Guide for Families and Friends of Chemically Dependent Persons.*

Leite, Evelyn, and Pamela Espeland. *Different Like Me: A Book for Teens Who Worry About Their Parents' Use of Alcohol/Drugs.*

Schaefer, Dick. *Choices & Consequences: What to Do When A Teenager Uses Alcohol/Drugs—A Step-by-Step System That Really Works.*

Wilmes, David. *Parenting for Prevention: How to Raise a Child to Say No to Alcohol/Drugs—For Parents, Teachers, and Other Concerned Adults.*

## Workbooks

Sassatelli, Jean, R.N. *Breaking Away: Saying Goodbye to Alcohol/Drugs—A Guide to Help Teenagers Stop Using Chemicals.*

Zarek, David, and James Sipe. *Can I Handle Alcohol/Drugs? A Self-Assessment Guide for Youth.*


## Booklets

*Alcoholism: A Treatable Disease.*

Anderson, Gary L. *Enabling in the School Setting.*

Anderson, Gary L. *Solving Alcohol/Drug Problems in Your School.*

*Chemical Dependence and Recovery: A Family Affair.*

*Chemical Dependence: Yes, You Can Do Something.*

Cloninger, Robert. *Genetic and Environmental Factors Leading to Alcoholism.*

*The Family Enablers.*

Leite, Evelyn. *How It Feels to Be Chemically Dependent.*

Leite, Evelyn. *Detachment: The Art of Letting Go While Living with an Alcoholic.*

*Recovery of Chemically Dependent Families.*

*Why Haven't I Been Able to Help?*

## Periodicals

*Focus on the Family and Chemical Dependence*. 2119-A Hollywood Blvd., Hollywood, FL 33020.

*Student Assistance Journal*. P.O. Box 6282, Syracuse, NY 13217-7922.


## Films/Videocassettes

*Back to Reality*. Color, 33 minutes.

*Choices and Consequences: Intervention with Youth in Trouble with Alcohol/Drugs*. Color, 33 minutes.

*Different Like Me: For Teenage Children of Alcoholics*. Color, 31 minutes.

*Enabling: Masking Reality*. Color, 22 minutes.

*Intervention: Facing Reality*. Color, 30 minutes.

*Lots of Kids Like Us*. Color, 28 minutes. Gerald T. Rogers Productions.

*My Father's Son: The Legacy of Alcoholism*. Color, 33 minutes.

*Soft Is the Heart of a Child*. Color, 30 minutes. Hazelden Foundation.

*A Story About Feelings*. Color, 10 minutes.

*Where's Shelley?* Color, 13 minutes.


## Other

Black, Claudia. *The Stamp Game*. MAC Printing and Publications, 1850 High Street, Denver, CO 80218.

146

For more information or to order any of the Johnson Institute's printed materials, films, or videocassettes, call or write:

**Johnson Institute**
7151 Metro Boulevard
Minneapolis, MN 55435-3425
1-800-231-5165
In Minnesota, call 1-800-247-0484 or 944-0511
In Canada, call 1-800-447-6660

When ordering, be sure to request copies of the Johnson Institute's Publications and Films Catalogue and its Training Calendar.

## National Organizations

The following groups and organizations can provide additional information on preventing alcohol and other drug use by children and adolescents.

A.A.
Alcoholics Anonymous
General Service Office
P.O. Box 459
Grand Central Station
New York, NY 10163
(212) 686-1100

Addiction Research Foundation
33 Russell Street
Toronto, Ontario M5S 2S1, Canada
(416) 595-6056

Al-Anon Family Group Headquarters
1372 Broadway
New York, NY  10018-0862
(212) 302-7240

Alateen
1372 Broadway
New York, NY  10018-0862
(212) 302-7240

American Council for Drug Education
204 Monroe Street
Rockville, MD  20850
(301) 294-0600

Chemical People Project/WQED-TV
4802 Fifth Avenue
Pittsburgh, PA  15213
(412) 622-1491

COAF
Children of Alcoholics Foundation, Inc.
200 Park Avenue, 31st Floor
New York, NY  10166
(212) 351-2680

Families Anonymous
World Service Office
P.O. Box 528
Van Nuys, CA  91408
(818) 989-7841

Families in Action Drug Information Center
2296 Henderson Mill Road, Suite 204
Atlanta, GA 30345
(404) 325-5799

Hazelden Foundation
Box 11
Center City, MN 55012
1-800-328-9000

IBCA
Institute on Black Chemical Abuse
2614 Nicollet Avenue South
Minneapolis, MN 55408
(612) 871-7878

Johnson Institute
7151 Metro Boulevard
Minneapolis, MN 55435
1-800-231-5165

National Association for Children of Alcoholics, Inc.
(NACOA)
31582 Coast Highway, Suite B
South Laguna, CA 92677-3044
(714) 499-3889

Narcotics Anonymous (NA)
World Services Office, Inc.
P.O. Box 9999
Van Nuys, CA 91409
(818) 780-3951

National Coalition for the Prevention
of Drug and Alcohol Abuse
537 Jones Road
Granville, OH 43023
(614) 587-2800

National Federation of Parents
for Drug-Free Youth
8730 Georgia Avenue, Suite 200
Silver Spring, MD 20910
(301) 585-5437

National Council on Alcoholism (NCA)
12 West 21st Street, 7th Floor
New York, NY 10010
1-800-NCA-CALL

National Clearinghouse for Alcohol/Drug Information
(NCADI)
P.O. Box 2345
Rockville, MD 28052
(301) 468-2600

National Institute on Alcohol Abuse and Alcoholism
(NIAAA)
Room 16-105, Parklawn Building
5600 Fishers Lane
Rockville, MD 20857
(301) 443-3885

National Institute on Drug Abuse (NIDA)
 Room 10-05, Parklawn Building
5600 Fishers Lane
Rockville, MD  20857
(301) 443-6480

National Parents Resource Institute on Drug Education
(PRIDE)
Robert W. Woodruff Volunteer Service Center, Suite 1002
100 Edgewood Avenue
Atlanta, GA  30303
(404) 651-2548

Students Against Drunk Driving (SADD)
P.O. Box 800
277 Main Street
Marlboro, MA  01752
1-800-521-SADD

# Appendix

## The Twelve Steps*

1. We admitted we were powerless over alcohol—that our lives had become unmanageable.
2. Came to believe that a Power greater than ourselves could restore us to sanity.
3. Made a decision to turn our will and our lives over to the care of God *as we understood Him.*
4. Made a searching and fearless moral inventory of ourselves.
5. Admitted to God, to ourselves, and to another human being the exact nature of our wrongs.
6. Were entirely ready to have God remove all these defects of character.
7. Humbly asked Him to remove our shortcomings.
8. Made a list of all persons we had harmed, and became willing to make amends to them all.
9. Made direct amends to such people wherever possible, except when to do so would injure them or others.
10. Continued to take personal inventory and when we were wrong promptly admitted it.
11. Sought through prayer and meditation to improve our conscious contact with God *as we understood him,* praying only for knowledge of his will for us and the power to carry that out.
12. Having a spiritual awakening as a result of these steps, we tried to carry this message to alcoholics, and to practice these principles in all our affairs.

---

* From *Alcoholics Anonymous, Third Edition* (New York: Alcoholics Anonymous World Services, Inc., 1976), p. 59. Reprinted with permission of Alcoholics Anonymous World Services, Inc.

# JOHNSON INSTITUTE

When the Johnson Institute first opened its doors in 1966, few people knew or believed that alcoholism was a disease. Fewer still thought that anything could be done to help the chemically dependent person other than to wait for him or her to "hit bottom" and then pick up the pieces.

We've spent over twenty years spreading the good news that chemical dependence is a *treatable* disease. Through our publications, films, video and audiocassettes, and our training and consultation services, we've given hope and help to hundreds of thousands of people across the country and around the world. The intervention and treatment methods we've pioneered have restored shattered careers, healed relationships with co-workers and friends, saved lives, and brought families back together.

Today the Johnson Institute is an internationally recognized leader in the field of chemical dependence intervention, treatment, and recovery. Individuals, organizations, and businesses, large and small, rely on us to provide them with the tools they need. Schools, universities, hospitals, treatment centers, and other healthcare agencies look to us for experience, expertise, innovation, and results. With care, compassion, and commitment, we will continue to reach out to chemically dependent persons, their families, and the professionals who serve them.

To find out more about us, write or call:

7151 Metro Boulevard
Minneapolis, Mn 55435
1-800-231-5165
In MN: 1-800-247-0484
or 944-0511
In CAN: 1-800-447-6660

Need a copy for a friend? You may order directly.
## CONDUCTING SUPPORT GROUPS FOR STUDENTS AFFECTED BY CHEMICAL DEPENDENCE
### A Guide for Educators and Other Professionals
by Martin Fleming
Johnson Institute Book
$12.95

# Order Form

Please send _____ copy (copies) of **CONDUCTING SUPPORT GROUPS FOR STUDENTS AFFECTED BY CHEMICAL DEPENDENCE.**

Price $12.95 per copy. Please add $1.50 shipping for the first book and 50¢ for each additional copy.

_____
*Name (please print)*

_____
*Address*

_____
*City/State/Zip*

*Attention*
**Please note that orders under $75.00 must be prepaid.**
If paying by credit card, please
complete the following:

☐ Bill the full payment to my credit card.

☐ VISA ☐ MasterCard ☐ American Express

Credit card number: _____

For MASTERCARD
Write the 4 digits below the account number: _____

Expiration date: _____

Signature on card: _____

For faster service, call our Order Department
TOLL-FREE:
**1-800-231-5165**
In Minnesota call:
**1-800-247-0484**
or **(612) 944-0511**
In Canada call:
**1-800-447-6660**

Return this order form to:     The Johnson Institute
7151 Metro Boulevard
Minneapolis, MN 55435-3425
Ship to (if different from above):

_____
*Name (please print)*

_____
*Address*

_____
*City/State/Zip*